Con. Research   Mar. 1 7 1965

Santa Clara County Free Library

REFERENCE

 58 1 6

Pacific
COASTAL LINERS

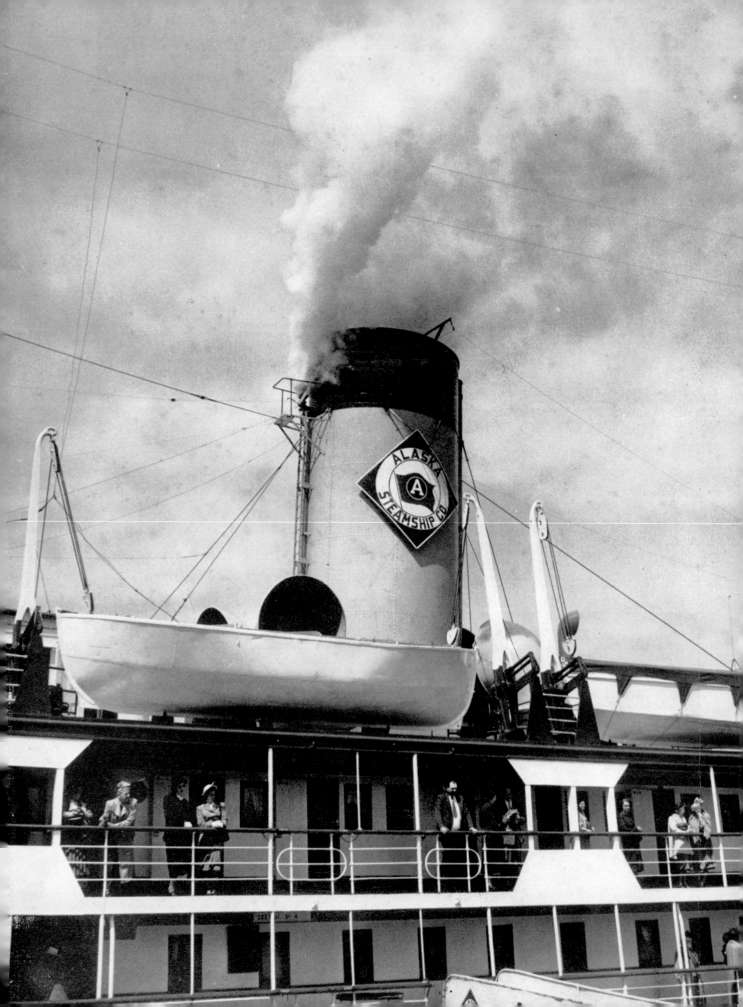

Pacific
COASTAL LINERS

By Gordon Newell & Joe Williamson

SUPERIOR PUBLISHING COMPANY·SEATTLE

The throaty voice of a coastal liner, left, warns tardy passengers that sailing time is near.
Wheeling sea gulls escort the Queen, above, as she churns her way up the California coast.

With smoke-billowing stacks and trailing lines, white racer YALE leaves San Francisco docks for turbine driven run to Los Angeles.

Dedication

To Captain Joshua Green, Senior, who has been intimately associated with West Coast shipping for more than seventy years, partly because of his major contributions to the preservation of maritime history, but mostly because, at the age of ninety, he is possessed of a heart which is both warm and young.

Foreword

As in the previous books of this West Coast maritime series, *Pacific Tugboats* and *Pacific Steamboats*, this volume is designed primarily for the reader's pleasure rather than his education. It seeks to convey the flavor and the color of an era and does not pretend to cover the complete and detailed history of that era.

The memory of the coastwise passenger liners is a blend of many things . . . the wind-whipped blare of the ship's band on sailing day and the brightly colored paper ribbons linking ship and pier. The reverberation of the whistle on a foggy night and the lazy roll of a whale, glimpsed briefly amid the profound swells of the North Pacific. The smell of the sea and the aroma of the steaming coffee in the steward's silver urn. And this memory is brushed with the extra magic of things now vanished which are reminiscent of younger, greener days.

If this memory is made more vivid to those who knew and loved the coastal liners, this book shall have fulfilled its purpose. The authors have not, however, made the informal nature of *Pacific Coastal Liners* an excuse for inaccurate reporting. Every effort has been made to keep the information in text and caption as authentic as possible. Mistakes will, of course, be found, for people who write books completely free of errors never get them finished. The serious student of Pacific Coast history may find the factual material herein too limited for his tastes, but he may be assured that it *is* factual.

Much credit for this must go to the many friends who helped provide material and information for the compiling of *Pacific Coastal Liners*, among them Puget Sound Maritime Historical Society researchers Lloyd M. Stadum and Robert C. Leithead, Lynn S. Whitman, youthful but devoted student of West Coast shipping, of Sacramento, Captain Floyd Smith of the Puget Sound pilots, Robert E. Matson, Roy Bruce, Albert N. Plush, Karl Kortum, director of the San Francisco Maritime Museum, Robert G. Manette, of the San Francisco offices of Union Steamship Company of New Zealand, H. J. Keeler, Wilbur Thompson and Sid G. Hayman, of the Alaska Steamship Company, Ivar Haglund, well-known Seattle seafood, song and shipping authority, Marine Digest editor James A. Gibbs, Jr., W. R. Beardsley, Pittsburg, Herbert H. Tiesler, Oakland, Clarence N. Rogers, San Bernardino, George R. Dennis, North Vancouver, B.C., Roseburg, Oregon Author G. B. Abdill, Seattle Artist James Allan and Capt. Kenneth N. Dodson, author of the best-selling *Away All Boats* and other outstanding maritime books.

Next year's volume in the Superior Publishing Company's maritime series will be titled *Pacific Lumber Ships*; will tell the story of the coastwise freighters, sail and steam, which carried the harvest of the forests, from grape-stakes and shingles to giant redwood timbers and Douglas fir logs, from British Columbia, Washington and Oregon to California.

Again we say, to those who have material on the coastwise steam schooners, sailing schooners, barkentines and other ships of the West Coast lumber fleet, you're welcome to join the crew of *Pacific Lumber Ships*.

Gordon Newell
Joe Williamson
Colman Ferry Terminal
Seattle 4, Washington

The **Spokane** gives Pacific seascape a banner of coal smoke. (Opposite)

LAST VOYAGE FOR A PRINCESS: Canadian Pacific's graceful three-stacker *Princess Elizabeth*, above, made her last run on the traditional Seattle-Victoria-Vancouver triangle run early in 1959. Foss tugs, ferries and other harbor craft in Seattle accorded her the three whistle-blast salute due retiring royalty.

Al Ki, left and **Aleutian,** right, were veteran Alaskan liners of different eras.

TALES OF GHOSTS AND GOLD are told of the old Alaska steamer **Humboldt**, above, which began voyaging north in the early days of the great Alaska gold rush, made a final strange voyage a generation later with no living hand at her wheel. (See page 108)

Princess Joan at Victoria, left. **H. F. Alexander** sweeps grandly down the Strait of Juan de Fuca, right.

A NIP AGAINST THE SEA CHILL could always be had at the bars of the coastal liners, except during the prohibition era. That pictured on the opposite page was on the Alaska Line's **Aleutian.**
Above, an Alaska Liner passes through the government locks at Seattle, en-route to winter layup in Lake Washington, while below, Alaska Line's **Baranof** skirts Taku Glacier in southern Alaska.

Next page: A seagull's-eye view of the **Victoria** furrowing the Bering Sea at thirteen knots.

CALIFORNIA COAST SAILINGS
SAN FRANCISCO
LOS ANGELES
SAN DIEGO

LASSCO
SERVICE

LASSCO
SERVICE

CALIFORNIA COAST SAILINGS
SAN FRANCISCO
LOS ANGELES
SAN DIEGO

1—1
5-1-33

YALE

MATSON LINE
LASSCO LINE
OCEANIC LINE

to HAWAII

and, via HONOLULU, SAMOA and FIJI
to NEW ZEALAND and AUSTRALIA

1—1
5-1-33

NORTHBOUND

Lv. San Diego (L. A. S. S. Co.) . . 10:00 A.M.	Mon.	SEE		
Ar. Wilmington . . . . 3:00 P.M.	Mon.	NOTE		
Ar. Los Angeles (P. E. Ry.) 1 hour after Ar. Wilmington	Mon.	BELOW		
Lv. Los Angeles (P. E. Ry.) . . . 4:00 P.M.	Mon.	Wed.	Fri.	
Lv. Wilmington (L. A. S. S. Co.) . 5:00 P.M.	Mon.	Wed.	Fri.	
Ar. San Francisco (Pier 32) . . . 11:00 A.M.	Tues.	Thurs.	Sat.	

SOUTHBOUND

Lv. San Francisco (Pier 32) . . . . 5:00 P.M.	Tues.	Thurs.	Sat.	
Ar. Wilmington . . . . 11:00 A.M.	Wed.	Fri.	Sun.	
Ar. Los Angeles (P. E. Ry.) 1 hour after Ar. Wilmington	Wed.	Fri.	Sun.	
Lv. Los Angeles (P. E. Ry.) . . . 2:00 P.M.	SEE		Sun.	
Lv. Wilmington (L. A. S. S. Co.) . 3:00 P.M.	NOTE		Sun.	
Ar. San Diego . . . . 8:00 P.M.	BELOW		Sun.	

THE PIONEERS

Scheduled coastwise steamship service came to the Pacific Coast of the United States with the California Gold Rush, but for the first couple of years — from 1849 until 1851 — it was strictly limited to the shuttling of treasure seekers between the Isthmus of Panama and San Francisco. Most of the 49'ers preferred the overland route across the isthmus to the long, hazardous voyage around Cape Horn. There were plenty of East Coast ships to transport them to the Atlantic side of the isthmus, but only a few plying the waters of the Pacific. Consequently anything that gave the slightest promise of remaining afloat for the voyage to San Francisco was besieged by eager passengers at Panama City.

This set an unfortunate pattern for Pacific Coast steamship service for the next half century. Shipowners who made fortunes running decrepit, overloaded old tubs up and down the coast during gold rush days saw no reason to change their tactics when gold rush hysteria gave way to solid growth and development along the new frontier. The custom of making the Pacific Coast a dumping ground for tender old hulks which had already lived out their normal life-spans on the Atlantic was to cost a great many human lives.

The first regularly scheduled liner to run north out of San Francisco was, however, a new, sturdy and respectable little brig-rigged side-wheeler. The *Columbia* was launched at New York in 1850, built especially for the California-Oregon coasting trade. She arrived on the West Coast in 1851 and was duly enrolled at the Astoria customs house as having "a round stern and eagle head, a length of 193 feet, six inches and a beam of 29 feet." The firm of Holland & Aspinwall operated her on a regular schedule between San Francisco and Portland. During the first five years of her service she completed 102 trips on this route, plus one to Panama, steaming 220,000 miles and hauling 80,000 tons of freight and 10,000 passengers.

The *Columbia* was a safe and dependable little ship and until 1853 she had things pretty much her own way along the North Pacific coast. Captain George Flavel of Astoria tried running competition to the *Columbia* with the stubby side-wheeler *Goliah*, a boat with a history of biting off more than she could chew. Although remarkably slow, the *Goliah* was always challenging other craft to race and was invariably beaten soundly. Having been built as a towboat, she had ambitions of becoming a coastwise passenger liner, but her lack of both size and speed made her a poor match for the *Columbia* and she retired to a long career of tugboating on San Francisco Bay and Puget Sound. Her skipper, Captain Flavel, set up business as a Columbia River bar pilot, making a highly successful career of guiding other people's ships in and out of the mighty and highly treacherous River of the West.

Another of the *Columbia's* early competitors, the *General Warren*, was more typical of the negligent homicide school of navigation which was to make drowning a major item in Pacific Coast mortality tables.

The *General Warren* was a little wooden side-wheeler, built at Portland, Maine back in 1844. This 300-ton paddler wasn't designed for ocean voyaging when she was new and by 1852, when she began bucking the North Pacific in opposition to the *Columbia*, her hull was rotten and her engine wheezy.

Late on the afternoon of January 28, 1852, the *General Warren*, deeply loaded with grain and carrying a score of passengers, waddled ungracefully across the Columbia bar, paused briefly to drop pilot Flavel, then squared away toward San Francisco. Her single-cylindered engine clanked dolefully and huffed steam from numerous leaky joints as it worked against a rising south wind. The tired hull groaned to the thrust of vicious gray seas.

Toward midnight the foretopmast was carried away and the hull was leaking badly. Captain Charles Thompson brought her about and set his course back for the Columbia. The grain cargo had gotten into the bilges to choke the pumps and the overloaded steamer was slowly sinking. She reached the river mouth in the morning, but the pilot boat didn't come alongside until late in the afternoon. Captain Flavel came back aboard, still unaware of what a floating coffin he was piloting. He proposed to keep the *Warren* offshore until morning, for the tide was ebbing, the bar was breaking viciously and it was almost dark.

The sick and terrified passengers crowded around him, begging him to take the ship in immediately. Captain Thompson admitted that she might not last out a night at sea, so at five o'clock in the evening Flavel ordered the pilot schooner to follow in their wake and headed the wallowing *General Warren* toward the churning darkness of the bar. The pilot was horrified to find that the old paddler was completely unmanageable in the breaking seas off the river mouth. She refused to answer her helm and she could make no headway against the tide's ebb. In desperation, the *Governor Warren* was headed for the breakers on Clatsop Spit. She hit the beach at seven in the evening and within minutes the sea was breaking clear over her. By nine that night her decks aft of the foremast had been swept clean of masts, funnel, paddle-boxes and superstructure, but passengers and crew were still alive below decks.

By three o'clock in the morning it was obvious that the steamer's rotten hull would disintegrate within hours. The pilot schooner had lost her favorable wind off the bar and was somewhere back at sea, unaware of the disaster. Captain Thompson asked pilot Flavel to take charge of a small boat to be sent to Astoria for assistance. The terrified passengers refused to enter the boat in the face of the tremendous breakers which were then sweeping the wreck, but Captain Flavel and a crew of ten volunteers got safely away and into Astoria, where they found the bark *George and Martha* at anchor. Captain Beard, the bark's master, dispatched a big whaleboat immediately to the scene of the wreck, but when the would-be rescuers arrived they found only the angry seas breaking unimpeded on Clatsop Spit. Not a vestige of the steamship *General Warren* remained. At daylight the melancholy work of collecting the scattered bodies of the more than thirty dead began along the rain-drenched beaches of the Columbia's mouth.

The *General Warren* had gained first place in what was to become a long roll of lost steam ships along the coast of the Pacific. Like many that were to follow, her shattered timbers were a sad monument to the greed of shipowners who valued extra profits above human lives.

In 1853 the Pacific Mail Steamship Company, its coffers bulging with gold rush profits from the San Francisco-Panama trade, bought out the interests of the pioneer northwest line, Holland & Aspinwall. Pacific Mail continued the *Columbia* on the northern run, adding their side-wheeler *Fremont* to extend the service to

PADDLE STEAMER OREGON entered Pacific Mail Line's San Francisco-Panama service early in 1849, carried first mail from continental United States to gold rush San Francisco. In later years she operated under sail in the coastwise lumber trade out of Seabeck, Washington.

HUDSON'S BAY STEAMER Labouchere was built at Green's Yard, Blackwall, London in 1858, arrived at Victoria the following year and made frequent coastwise voyages between British Columbia and San Francisco until 1866, when she struck a reef near San Francisco and sank with the loss of two lives.

Puget Sound in what had just become Washington Territory. Steilacoom, the largest village on the Sound, became the northern terminus for the Pacific Mail steamers. The *Fremont* also stopped off for two round trips a month on the Umpqua River.

The entry of the Pacific Mail line in the northern shipping business was a blow to the citizens of Portland, which was well on its way toward becoming the metropolis of the Pacific Northwest. Like other transportation companies before and since, Pacific Mail was determined to build a new city of its own to serve as its terminal port, thus adding the profits of land speculation to those of shipping. The steamship company expended considerable money in constructing wharf and warehouse facilities at St. Helens, 28 miles below Portland, and refused to send their steamers any further up the river.

In true pioneer spirit, the aroused Portlanders brought in the opposition steamer *Peytonia* to run between their town and San Francisco. The following year, 1854, Pacific Mail added the *Republic* to its Northwest fleet and the Portland-backed independent line countered by placing the *America* in service as running-mate for *Peytonia*. A spirited rivalry continued between the two lines, complete with rate wars and races, until Pacific Mail gave up its St. Helens scheme and resumed operations up the Willamette River to Portland.

At this period the San Francisco - Panama run, while not as lucrative as in gold rush days, was still the Pacific Mail line's primary coastal service. The older and less seaworthy vessels of its fleet were usually diverted to the secondary northern service. One of these was the old Panama liner *Isthmus,* a veteran paddler of 1847 vintage, which was renamed *Southerner* and placed on the San Francisco-Puget Sound run in 1854. She didn't last long, her last days being recorded with seamanlike brevity by her master, Captain F. A. Sampson:

"At Eureka December 22d. At Crescent City December 23d. Unable to get in at Port Orford or Umpqua, so went on for the Columbia. Passed Tillamook Head at 10:00 a.m. December 25; off Columbia bar at 1:00 p.m., with heavy S.W. swell. Engines out of line and racked by the swell; leaking. Lay by until 6:00 p.m., and, as could not get in, ran for Puget Sound with all pumps working. At 10:00 p.m. (water) gaining so fast that passengers had to bail with buckets and throw cargo overboard. Kept water down to engine room floor. December 26th at daylight sighted land 26 miles south of Cape Flattery; engines working very slowly; stood along the coast close hauled to wind until 4:00 p.m., when leak gained too fast and stern began to drop. Ran in 10 miles southeast of Cape Flattery and anchored in seven fathoms; sandy beach under lee. Seas broke over and she dragged; slipped chains and went on broadside. Cut away mast and smokestack, and the tide fell and left her quiet. At daylight, everybody got ashore safely, and, the sea rising, she soon went to pieces."

The 19 crew members and 28 passengers of the *Southerner* had a cheerless Christmas that winter of 1854, but they were more fortunate than many of their contemporaries. Theirs was a shipwreck from which they walked away.

More competition came to the northern sea route when, in 1857, John T. Wright placed the big side-wheeler *Commodore* in opposition to the Pacific Mail steamers under the houseflag of the Merchants' Accomodation Line. This resulted in another rate war to delight the hearts of the traveling public and an epic race between the *Columbia* and the *Commodore*, dur-

GENERAL MILES, left, and Alliance, right, were units of the Oregon & Coast Steamship Company, which served the smaller Northwest ports in the 1880's.

PACIFIC MAIL STEAMSHIP COMPANY sidewheeler **Dakota** looms large among Puget Sound small craft at Yesler's wharf, Seattle in 1875. **Dakota**, with the **City of Panama**, handled Pacific Mail's California-Pacific Northwest route for almost a decade.

ing which the two side-wheelers kept each other in sight all the way from the Golden Gate to the Columbia. The *Commodore*[1] soon reverted to her original name, *Brother Jonathan*, while Wright added the side-wheeler *Pacific* to run with her. The *Brother Jonathan* and *Pacific* were destined to become victims of two separate marine disasters which, for many years, made their names synonymous with horror and death. Fortunately for the good name of John Wright, he had unloaded his two ill-starred old hulks on the California Steam Navigation Company before they took their grizzly place in West Coast history.

[1] As a part of the British Columbia Centennial celebration during the summer of 1958, a Canadian naval vessel was converted into a replica of the old **Commodore**, replete with dummy sidewheels and funnel, and went splashing about Puget Sound scaring the daylights out of bibulous yachtsmen and fishermen, who thought they were seeing a ghost. The **Commodore** brought the first consignment of Fraser River gold miners to Victoria in 1858.

The California Steam Navigation Company, which had hitherto confined its operations largely to bay and river runs in the San Francisco area, entered the coastal service in 1858 as the result of another gold rush, this one in the north. Gold had been discovered on the Fraser River of British Columbia and there was a rush of freight and passenger traffic to the ports nearest to the gold fields. The result was a record number of scheduled steamers running north from San Francisco. The fleet of 1858 included the *Orizaba, Cortez, Oregon, Sierra Nevada* and *Panama* of Pacific Mail, *Pacific* and *Brother Jonathan* of California Steam, and the independent *Santa Cruz*. During this era Canada had no coastal steamships to place in line service, although the old Hudson's Bay propeller *Otter* made occasional coastwise voyages hauling British Columbia cranberries and coal to the San Francisco market.

THE PIONEERS

Left, top to bottom: **Columbia**, 193-foot paddler, inaugurated scheduled San Francisco-Portland service in 1851. **Republic** joined the **Columbia** in Pacific Mail service to Oregon in 1854. **California**, newly launched at New York, was on her way around Cape Horn when gold was discovered in California. She was the first American steamship to round the Horn and join the gold rush.

Right, top to bottom: **Brother Jonathan**, also served West Coast routes under name of **Commodore**, her career ending in disaster in 1865. **Northerner** struck Blunt's Reef off the California coast in 1860; was also lost with heavy death toll. **Oriflamme**, built as a Civil War gunboat, became the West Coast flagship of transportation mogul Ben Holladay. **Gussie Telfair**, a fast, propeller-driven blockade runner during the Civil War, served routes from Alaska to California from 1869 until 1880, when she was wrecked off Coos Bay.

PADDLING SMARTLY NORTH, Pacific Coast Steamship Company's side-wheeler **Ancon** was a pioneer on the San Francisco-Puget Sound-Alaska run. She stranded and sank at Loring, Alaska in 1883.

Having drained the profits of two major gold rushes, the Pacific Mail Steamship Company withdrew from the coastwise trade in 1861, concentrating on its trans-Pacific service. The pioneer company's northern line was sold to a new shipping firm, the California, Oregon & Mexican Steamship Company. This was the salt water link in the Western transportation network of Ben Holladay, designed to connect with his river steamers on the Columbia and his Overland Stage Line at Wallulla. Holladay took over from Pacific Mail the steamers *Cortez, Oregon, Sierra Nevada, Republic,* and *Panama*[2] and operated them amiably with the California Steam Navigation Company's. Both Holladay

and the leading lights of California Steam were cold-blooded realists who were fully aware that rate wars and races were more spectacular than profitable. They preferred a good, old-fashioned conspiracy to fix rates. They set cabin fares between San Francisco and Portland at $45.00. Those who weren't too particular about food and accommodations could go steerage at $25.00.

This happy arrangement continued for several years, but in 1866 a Maine Yankee named Patton upset the corporate apple carts of California Steam and the California, Oregon & Mexico Steamship Company. Bringing out the big side-wheeler *Montana* from New England, he hoisted the house flag of the Anchor Line and set about making life miserable for the big companies. Rates quickly fell to $20 first class and $10.00 steerage; then to the unheard-of low of ten and three dollars.

[2] The **Panama** was one of the first three steamers to round Cape Horn and enter Pracific Coast service between San Francisco and Panama. She came out, along with the **Oregon** and **California**, in 1849.

SETTING A PATTERN for later day Alaska excursionists, the passengers of the **Ancon** gathered atop a convenient deckhouse to have their picture immortalized on the glass plate negative of an 1880 maritime photographer. All hands were apparently enjoying their cruise except the little gentleman in the front row right, who seems to have been suffering from a toothache.

The new company was somewhat handicapped by its one-ship status, but Patton announced stoutly that he was having another steamer, the *Idaho*, rushed to completion in Maine. There was a great deal of travel along the Pacific Coast during this era, but no profit for any of the steamship companies. Unable to scare the stubborn Patton off, Holladay offered financial terms which no self-respecting New Englander could turn down. The eventual result was the North Pacific Transportation Company, a combination of the California Steam Navigation Company, Holladay's California, Oregon & Mexico Steamship Company and Patton's Anchor Line. Rates, needless to say, went up to their previous levels and by 1869 the North Pacific Transportation Company was operating ten side-wheelers and six propeller steamers north from San Francisco. Its fleet included the *Active*, *John L. Stephens*, *Moses Taylor* (known to her passengers as *Rolling Moses*), *Oriflamme*, *Orizaba*, *Pacific*, *Panama*, *Senator*, *Sierra Nevada*, *Ajax*, *California*, *Continental*, *Gussie Telfair*, *Idaho*, *Montana* and *Pelican*.

The *Continental* was a fine big ex-government transport built solidly of oak and hickory. She gained a lasting place in history as the ship which transported the legendary Mercer Girls around Cape Horn to Seattle. The wily Holladay fast-talked Asa Mercer into turning the *Continental* over to him, after which he charged him a thumping fee to transport his cargo of prospective brides west, fed the unfortunate girls largely on boiled beans and finally dumped them unceremoniously in San Francisco, a thousand miles from their waiting suitors on Puget Sound. Poor Mercer, having spent all his own money and that of numerous friends, was driven from home in disgrace, but Holladay came out of the affair with a tidy profit and a fine new steamship.

Holladay's favorite ship, however, was the *Oriflamme*, which had been built in 1864 as a fast naval gunboat and had subsequently engaged in the China coastal trade. Although ostensibly a unit of his coastwise fleet, the *Oriflamme* was used as a private yacht by the flambouyant Holladay and some epic parties were held in her cabins, some lasting all the way from San Francisco to Alaska.

In the meantime, the toll of western shipwrecks had continued to mount. Panama Mail's *Northerner* had left San Francisco with 108 passengers and crew on January 4, 1860. Her destination was the Columbia River and Puget Sound. She didn't make it.

Paddling up the coast at a good twelve-knot clip, she brushed rather lightly over an outlying and uncharted rock at Blunt's Reef off Cape Mendocino. The impact, almost unnoticed by passengers and crew, was sufficient to open up the side-wheeler's overworked timbers. Soon all pumps were working, syphoning out 12,000 gallons of cold sea water a minute, but the water was rising in the holds at the rate of an inch a minute. Amid this precariously balanced state of affairs, Captain W. L. Dall set the old *Northerner* on a course toward the shelter of Humboldt Bay. Off Cape Fortunas the engineer informed the captain that the water was over the engine room floor plates and the boiler fires would soon be out.

With no other alternative, Captain Dall headed the sinking paddler toward the beach. Her progress was agonizingly slow. It took the engine a full three seconds to make a single revolution, and the weight of the water in her holds pressed her down mercilessly. Deep in the water, the *Northerner* stranded well off shore and was immediately smothered by breaking seas. During a brief lull the first mate got a lifeboat away with most of the women passengers aboard, but the next two boats were capsized and most of their occupants drowned.

Chief Engineer Thomas O'Neil swam to shore with a line, which he made fast on the beach, but most of the remaining passengers were too terrified to attempt a hand-over-hand journey above the raging breakers. Forward an ingenious seaman somehow coaxed a terrified horse from the 'tween-decks, got it overboard and, firmly grasping its tail, was safely towed ashore. Finally, when it was apparent that the *Northerner* was in the last stages of dissolution, Captain Dall, the pilot and purser swung themselves ashore by way of the chief engineer's lifeline.

It seemed that the remaining ship's company were doomed, but in the ship's final moments a huge section of deck, with most of the terrified passengers on it, broke loose and drifted ashore as if guided by the very hand of God. Thus a

TRAGIC NIGHT. Death claimed 38 of the steamship **Northerner's** company when she struck a reef off Cape Mendocino in the pre-dawn darkness of January 4, 1860.

complete disaster was averted, only 38 of the more than one hundred persons aboard the *Northerner* being drowned. The Pacific Mail Steamship Company was well on its way toward setting a shipwreck record.[3]

It was worse when the *Brother Jonathan*, formerly the *Commodore*, hit St. George Reef off the California coast in July of 1865. Only 19 of her complement of 185 survived. The *Brother Jonathan* had nearly foundered at sea with 350 passengers aboard back in 1858, after which John Wright had wisely sold her to the California Steam Navigation Company, in whose service she was running when final disaster struck her.

California Steam, noted for its blithe disregard of human life where profits were involved, was doing a handsome business between San Francisco, Victoria and Puget Sound in 1865. Freight was piling up on the San Francisco dock faster than the line's coastwise steamers could haul it north. The aging *Brother Jonathan* was crammed with freight until her holds bulged. Then more was piled on deck. Captain Samuel De Wolfe stormed ashore to inform the company's agent that the steamer was being dangerously overloaded. The agent told him that if he was too timid to take the *Brother Jonathan* to sea there were a dozen jobless captains along the waterfront who would be glad to do so at a moment's notice. Captain De Wolfe went back aboard and at noon on July 28 the *Brother Jonathan* staggered away from her dock, festooned with freight and listing drunkenly.

Off the Farralones she fell in with a gale from the northwest and was barely able to make steerage way against it. Two days later she was off Crescent City and the gale had risen to such proportions that she was unable to make any headway at all. The captain put her about in an attempt to reach shelter at Crescent

3 A total of 31 Pacific Mail steamships were wrecked between 1853 and 1915, all but two in the Pacific. Nearly two thousand lives were lost in these disasters.

LEGENDARY SEA DISASTER of the Pacific Coast claimed 277 lives when, in 1875, the old side-wheeler **Pacific** rammed a square-rigged ship off Cape Flattery and sank within a few horror-filled minutes. Early day newspapers told the tragic news in extras like the one reproduced at the right.

City. Soon thereafter the *Brother Jonathan* crashed into submerged Northwest Seal Rock, an outlying fang of St. George Reef. Within minutes the ship's keel fell off and floated to the surface, the foremast plunged through the deck and the rotten hull began to open up like a ripe melon.

Confusion was rampant. Lifeboats were swamped by panic-stricken passengers and only one, carrying the 19 survivors, escaped from the wreckage. When the broken hulk was swept off the reef, Captain De Wolfe went down with 165 of his ship's company, cursing the greed and stupidity of the company that had forced him to take the overloaded old side-wheeler into the teeth of a North Pacific gale. The 19 survivors were picked up by the steamer *Del Norte*. Some 75 bodies were later found along the coast. No sign of the *Brother Jonathan*, her other victims, or of a quarter of a million dollar Army payroll she was carrying, were ever seen again.

The *Brother Jonathan's* sister hoodoo-ship, the *Pacific*, lasted until 1875, but when she went the toll was still more shocking. Carrying about

Washington Standard.

EXTRA.

Loss of the St'p Pacific
OFF CAPE FLATTERY !

Fearful Loss of Life !

TWENTY PASSENGERS FROM THE SOUND ABOARD THE

ILLFATED CRAFT

By W. U. Telegraph from the Regular Correspondent of the Standard.

PORT TOWNSEND, Nov. 7, 1875.

The American ship Messenger, Capt. V. E. Gilkey, has just arrived here, nine days from San Francisco. She reports having picked up a part of a pilot-house 20 miles south of Cape Flattery, containing Henry L. Jelly, the only survivor of the steamship *Pacific* which sailed from Victoria at 9 A. M. Thursday morning and foundered 40 miles south of Cape Flattery at 8 P. M. Thursday night. Mr. Jelly floated on the pilot-house from 8 o'clock Thursdao night until 10 A. M. Saturday morning, when he was picked up by the *Messenger*. Several boats were launched but all foundered.

The *Pacific* had the following passengers from the Sound:

From Tacoma—J. Hellmute and wife, Mrs. Mahon and child, H. C. Victor, J. T. Vining, Fred. D. Hard.

From Seattle—C. B. Davidson and wife, A. Robins, T Allison, O McPherson, Wm Maxwell, D. Woods.

From Victoria—F. Garesche, Miss A. Reynolds, Miss F. Palmer, Mrs. Lawson, Mrs. Moote, Mrs. S. T. Styles and child, D. C. McIntire, C. B. Fiarbanks, Captain and Mrs. Parsons, A. B. Oadway, W. J. Ferry, J. F. Johnston, Thos. Smith, John Cochrane, S. P. Moody, T. J. Farrell, M. Summers, C. Summers, J. Cahill, John Watson, E. H. Polley, Cal. Mandeville, wife and child, R. Hudson, H. Clime, E. P. Atkins, Thos Bevelry, R. Layzell, W. Waldron, John Lee, G. Gribbell, Geo. Morton, John McCormick, John Sampson, Wm. Wills, A. Lang, John G. Todd, Jas. Lenning, P. L. Chapman, Jas. H. Webbs, Isaac Webb.s

There were upwards of 200 passengers aboard the ill-fated craft.

ALASKA EXCURSIONS

Season 1906

"Totem Pole Route"—Land of the Midnight Sun

Summer Days		Glaciers
And Winter Scenes	PACIFIC COAST STEAMSHIP CO.	Totems and a
During		Thousand
A Trip to Alaska		Islands En Route

INSIDE PASSAGE—SEA SICKNESS UNKNOWN

STEAMSHIP "SPOKANE"

The Palatial Alaska Excursion Steamship "**SPOKANE**" Will Leave Tacoma, Seattle and Victoria

June 7, 21, July 5, 20, August 2

230 people, the *Pacific* sailed from Victoria, headed for San Francisco, on November 4. At ten that night she rammed the square-rigged ship *Orpheus,* north-bound for Puget Sound. The blow was not a heavy one, certainly not great enough to have seriously damaged a well-found ship. But the tender old *Pacific* fell apart at the seams and sank like a stone in a matter of minutes. The *Orpheus,* somewhat damaged herself, drifted off in the darkness, her crew unaware of the *Pacific's* dissolution. Eventually she piled up on the rocks off the Vancouver Island coast, but no lives were lost.

Of the *Pacific's* 230 passengers and crew, only two survivors were picked up, clinging to bits of wreckage. One of these died shortly thereafter as a result of shock and exposure.

In that same year of 1875, the Pacific Mail Steamship Company, having earlier reclaimed its ships from a bankrupt Holladay, sold out to Goodall, Nelson & Perkins Steamship Company, although another new firm, the Oregon Steamship Company had gained control of the old Holladay boats *Oriflamme, John L. Stephens, Gussie Telfair* and *Ajax.*

In 1877 Goodall and Perkins reorganized their company as the Pacific Coast Steamship Company. Their emblem, a red Maltese cross, was to remain dominant on the coastal sea lanes of the North Pacific for more than half a century.

TRANSPORTATION MAGNATE Ben Holladay, left, virtually controlled West Coast shipping in 1860's and early seventies.

LATER ERA in Alaska travel is depicted by passengers posing on the steamship **Tacoma** during a 1904 voyage. Captain Connauton is in the center of the group in uniform. The lady in the king-size fur coat is identified as a Mrs. Baber, the seated figure as "Count Padorski, the Polish Russian." . . . **Beardsley Collection**

PACIFIC COAST STEAM

With the strong restraining hand of Ben Holladay gone from the West Coast transportation scene, the two dominant steamship companies, the Oregon Steamship Company and Goodall & Perkins' Pacific Coast Company, started fighting for the coastal trade in an old-fashioned, knock-down-and-drag-out transportation war.

In 1877 the Pacific Coast Steamship Company had the larger fleet, composed of the side-wheelers *Ancon, Senator, Orizaba* and *Mahongo* and the propellers *Los Angeles, San Luis, Santa Cruz, Monterey, Gypsy, Donald, Salinas, Idaho, San Vincent* and *Constantine*. In opposition to Pacific Steam's 14-ship fleet, Oregon Steam had only six vessels in operation, the side-wheelers *Oriflamme* and *John L. Stephens* and the propellers *Gussie Telfair, Ajax, George W. Elder* and *City of Chester*. However, the 1200-ton iron propellers *George W. Elder* and *City of Chester*[1] were the fastest and most modern liners on the coast, inaugurating a five-day round-trip schedule between Portland and San Francisco.

During the course of this first year in Pacific Coast Steamship Company's history, a savage rate war with Oregon Steam slashed passenger fares between the Golden Gate and the Columbia River to an all-time low of $7.50 and three dollars.

So ruinous was this rivalry between the two companies that a truce was declared the follow-ing year, with fares returning to normal. They didn't stay that way long, however, for P. B. Cornwall of San Francisco came charging into the fray with his side-wheel monster, *Great Republic*.

The *Great Republic* was one of the last of the Pacific Mail Steamship Company's wooden side-wheelers, built on Long Island in 1866. A huge ship for her type, she was 378 feet long and registered at 3,882 tons. Although constructed of copper-fastened white oak and chestnut, she proved no match for the stormy seas she met with in the Mail Line's China service; furthermore, she consumed astounding amounts of coal and was not popular with the more up-to-date travelers. Side-wheelers were going out of style.

In view of her infirmities, Pacific Mail sold the *Great Republic* to Cornwall at a bargain price. Waterfront rumor had it that the new owner planned to use the *Great Republic* without the expense of actually operating her. It was common practice in those days for established shipping companies to pay rival owners a handsome subsidy to keep their vessels out of service and tied up at some convenient dock.

The Pacific Coast and Oregon Steamship companies refused to go along with Mr. Cornwall's venture into legalized maritime blackmail, so he made good his threat by the expensive process of getting up steam in the *Great Republic's* boilers. He further annoyed the big companies by setting San Francisco-Portland fares at the unheard-of low price of seven dollars first class and two dollars steerage. Freight was carried for $1.50 a ton. The two established lines vowed to drive this upstart out of business and forthwith lowered their rates to meet those of the *Great Republic*. Cornwall countered by lowering fares to four and two dollars, with freight at a dollar a ton. The other companies, having set a precedent, sadly followed suit.

1 The **Elder** which, in her old age bore the humiliating nickname of **George W. Roller**, lived a long and varied life. Although she struck a rock in the Columbia River near Rainier, Oregon on January 21, 1905 and lay submerged until May 22, 1906, she remained active until after World War 1. Late in 1918 the Tacoma Ledger reported "the ancient steamer" bound for Puget Sound from South America with a cargo of nitrates. At that time she was being operated by Captain Tom Crowley of San Francisco. Her old running-mate, the **City of Chester** ran afoul of the trans-Pacific liner **Oceanic** during a San Francisco Bay tule fog in August, 1888. She sank permanently, with the loss of 13 lives.

QUEEN OF THE PACIFIC was the original name of this famous Pacific coastal liner when she was launched at Philadelphia in 1882, but in a later and less expansive age it was shortened to Queen. Although involved in a great deal of Western history and numerous strandings, fires and minor catastrophies, she remained a popular, beautiful and respected ship until just before World War 2, when she was sold to Japanese scrappers.
Great Republic, below, carried San Francisco excursionists at cut rates to a shipwreck at the mouth of the Columbia River.

It was a frustrating experience, for Cornwall actually made money with his side-wheeler, while the big companies were doing their book keeping in red ink. Thousands of happy tourists flocked to the waterfront, carpet bags in hand, for it was much cheaper to travel on the coastwise liners than to stay at home in a dull boarding house. The *Great Republic* could cram aboard more than eight hundred of them to a voyage, with the result that even the ridiculously low fares more than paid the high costs of her operation. The smaller steamers of Pacific Coast and Oregon Steamship companies were unable to haul enough freight and passengers to pay their way.

Mr. Cornwall's troublesome enterprise was terminated suddenly in mid-April of 1879, when the *Great Republic* came paddling up to the Columbia bar at midnight, carrying 550 cabin and 346 steerage passengers from San Francisco. It was such a pleasant night that Captain Carroll decided to take the big side-wheeler over the bar that night instead of awaiting daylight. The pilot schooner came alongside to put pilot Doig aboard and he agreed that a night crossing shouldn't be particularly dangerous.

But the pilot failed to get proper bearings on low-lying Sand Island, just inside the river mouth. On the very crest of the flood tide, the *Great Republic* steamed majestically onto the beach. The steamer was not much damaged by the stranding, but as the tide fell the wooden hull was strained, twisting the engine out of line and making the pumps inoperative.

All the passengers were gotten safely to Astoria, but the next high tide flooded the helpless ship, after which a series of spring storms began the work of tearing her slowly to pieces.

SEATTLE-SAN FRANCISCO SHUTTLE service was long the niche of the **Queen**, which sailed under both Pacific Coast Steamship and H. F. Alexander's Pacific Steamship Company houseflags. Here she takes on a capacity passenger load in the heyday of the coastal liners.

Los Angeles, below, was originally the revenue cutter **Wyanda.** After many years of service on California and Northern routes she was wrecked on Point Sur, California in 1894, with the loss of three lives.

Several days after the stranding a salvage party headed by first officer Jessen left the wreck in the teeth of a rising wind. In attempting to get away from the steamer's side, Jessen broke the steering oar. The boat swamped and Jessen, along with ten of his crew, met death in the churning waters of the river mouth.

Following this episode, amicable relations were restored along the Pacific coastal route. The day of the side-wheeler was almost ended and the two major companies began bringing out fine iron steamships from the East . . . the *Oregon, State of California* and *Columbia*[2] with-

2 Although many uncomplimentary things were said about her in later years when she added more names to the long roll of West Coast shipwreck victims, the **Columbia** was, in the early 1880's, the pride of the Pacific Coast. Built at Chester, Pennsylvania in 1879, she was an iron propeller steamer of 1,746 tons, 309 feet long. It was the proud boast of her owners that only once in the first 15 years of her operation was she more than one night at sea on the San Francisco-Portland run.

in months of the *Great Republic's* stranding. Within the next few years such fine ships as the *Mississippi, Umatilla, Walla Walla* and *Queen of the Pacific* were added to the coastwsie fleet, some of them proving their stamina by lasting, sometimes under a series of different names, until the very end of the coastwise passenger steamship era.

During the period between 1870 and 1890, most seacoast communities, from San Diego and Santa Barbara to Grays Harbor, depended

PACIFIC COAST STEAMSHIP COMPANY

Left, top to bottom: **Ancon** was Pacific Coast Steamship Company pioneer. **Idaho,** another veteran of the California-Puget Sound trade, was wrecked in the Strait of Juan de Fuca in 1883, the same year the **Ancon** was lost in Alaska. **Mexico,** shown at San Francisco wharf, caried poet Joaquin Miller to Alaska in gold rush days; was lost off the British Columbia coast in August, 1897 without loss of life.

Right, top to bottom: **Montana,** built at Bath, Maine in 1865, sailed under Ben Holladay's colors for several years and was scrapped at Sacramento about 1870. **Umatilla,** originally a coastwise collier, became a well known passenger carrier, her last years in Admiral Line service. **Cottage City** was built at Bath, Maine in 1890 for the New York-Portland, Maine service; was brought to the West Coast in 1899 for Seattle-Skagway gold rush trade. Wrecked at Cape Mudge, B.C. January, 1911. **City of Pueblo,** built at Philadelphia in 1881 for Ward Line's Havana service. Came west in 1899 for Pacific Coast Company's Seattle-San Francisco run, until replaced by **Governor** in 1907. Was speed queen of New York-Havana and Seattle-San Francisco runs in her day.

COASTAL LINERS

Left, top to bottom: **City of Topeka**, built at Chester, Pa. in 1884 for Atchison, Topeka and Santa Fe Railway, came west in 1886 for Pacific Coast Company service. Replaced the lost **Ancon** on Puget Sound-Alaska run until 1902, when she took the San Francisco-Humboldt run until 1919, when she went to Honolulu as the **Waimea**. **George W. Elder** was known to passengers as George W. Roller. **Senator** loads at Pacific Coast Company's Seattle pier for Nome voyage, a service in which she spent many years after her launching at San Francisco in 1898. **Walla Walla**, once a notorious smuggler, later figured in sensational shipwreck.

Right, top to bottom: **Gypsy**, old wooden propeller, was used by Pacific Mail as tug; operated by Pacific Coast Co. in San Francisco to San Diego and Rogue River, Oregon runs and on Puget Sound. **Willamette Valley**, built 1883 for Oregon-Pacific R.R. Co. service to Yaquinna, shown here in PCS service leaving Eureka in 1900; wrecked a few months later near St. Michael. **City of Seattle**, built at Philadelphia in 1890 as Puget Sound steamer. Placed in Alaska trade by Dodwell & Co. in 1898 and retained by Pacific Steamship Company until 1921, when sold to Miami Steamship Co. for East Coast service, in which she remained until just before World War 2.

PACIFIC COAST STEAM

Left, top to bottom: **Santa Rosa** was specially built for West Coast service with shallow draft to negotiate then shallow harbor bar at San Pedro. In 1904 given major overhaul and one of two funnels removed. Wrecked at Point Arguello, July, 1911. **Bonita** worked southern routes; seldom left California coastal waters; was sold to the Mexican government in 1926. **Columbia** was another old-timer from the East Coast; sank off the Mendocino coast in July, 1907, with heavy loss of life.

Right, top to bottom: **Valencia**, ex-Spanish War transport, was prominent in gold rush trade to Alaska. Stranded on Vancouver Island coast in January, 1906 while on California-Puget Sound service, with loss of 117 lives. **Governor**, a coal-burner when she was built in 1907, was noted for her pair of skyscraper funnels. Rammed and sunk off Port Townsend in April, 1921. **President** was near-sister to **Governor**, though with only one tall stack. Saw last service as Alaska Steam's **Columbia**. **Congress**, pride of the line in 1913, became a burned-out hulk three years later, was rebuilt and became Admiral Line's **Emma Alexander.**

DEATH OF A SHIP is dramatized by lonely watcher on Point Arguello cliffs as Pacific Coast Company's **Santa Rosa** is pounded to pieces by ocean breakers. "Lives Risked to Save Money," West Coast newspapers charged in reporting this disaster.
Earlier loss of line's **Columbia**, below, brought similar charges.

EIGHTEEN PAGES. SEATTLE, WASHINGTON, MONDAY EVENING, JULY 22, 1907. Price 1 Cent. Newsstands and Trains, 5 Cents.

151 MEN AND WOMEN ON STEAMSHIP COLUMBIA ARE LOST

STEAMSHIPS COLLIDE AND 151 PERSONS DROWN

Columbia Is Struck by San Pedro Off Mendocino Coast and Sinks Within Five Minutes—All Except Officers on Watch Are Asleep in Their Berths—Captain Doran Remains at Post and Goes Down With His Vessel—No Time to Get Out the Life Preservers

The Times Special Service.

SAN FRANCISCO, Monday, July 22.--In a collision between the passenger steamship Columbia and the steam schooner San Pedro off Shelter Cove, on the Mendocino coast, one hundred and fifty-one passengers lost their lives Saturday night. The Columbia sank and lies completely submerged in the deep waters of Shelter Cove.

Capt. P. A. Doran, master of the Columbia, stayed with his vessel and is among those lost. It is reported that every woman passenger went down with the ship.

The collision occurred at midnight when all on board save the lookout and officers on the bridge were asleep. The Columbia was ...ing north at an easy rate, having left here at noon Saturday. Suddenly out of the fog loomed the dark hull of the steam schooner San Pedro, southbound, evidently out of her course. Whistles were

Steamship Columbia, sunk by the San Pedro

four boats and two rafts with eighty-eight passengers from the doomed ship. All passengers below the hurricane deck and the engineering force at work in the hold of the vessel were given no chance for their lives, but were drowned like rats in a trap. Most of the passengers were women. They had retired early in the evening and must have been sound asleep at the time of the collision. From my personal observance I did not see a single woman saved.

Foggy at the Time.

"It was foggy at the time. We were proceeding. I think under a slow bell. The San Pedro, which sailed from Eureka lumber laden, was proceeding at a high rate of speed and it is my own belief that the consequences of the disaster rest entirely upon the shoulders

A life raft was launched with a number of the passengers on board.

The steamship Roanoke spoke the steamship George W. Elder and the latter had on board eighty-eight passengers and members of the crew of the Columbia which were taken off the steamship San Pedro.

The San Pedro lost her stem and was damaged considerably forward. Her mainmast was gone and her foremast sprung; her cargo was gone and she was in a water-logged condition. The Elder towed her to Eureka. The Roanoke picked up a body supposed to be Edward Butler and brought it to this city.

COLUMBIA HAD GONE DOWN.

The steam lumber schooner Daisy Mitchell arrived here this morning bringing one of the Columbia's life boats and a life raft. Capt. Schmitt, of the Mitchell, said:

"We were southbound from Willapa Harbor and reached the scene of the collision about 1:30 o'clock yesterday morning. The Columbia had gone to the bottom and not even the tops of her masts were visible. The steamer George W. Elder at that time was taking the San Pedro in tow. The Elder was getting the San Pedro's chain to her after chock as we came up. I hailed the Elder and asked her if she wanted any assistance from us. I got such a short answer that you would think I had offered an insult.

"The San Pedro's stem was smashed to splinters and it looked to me as though she had rammed her way ten feet into the Columbia's bow. The San Pedro was settling at that time and had a heavy list. She had lost considerable of her deck load of lumber. The sea was smooth. The water all around was littered with timbers, kegs and splintered wood. We saw two life rafts of the Columbia and a life boat. We picked up the boat and one of the rafts and brought them along.

SAW MANY LIFE PRESERVERS.

"We saw a great many life preservers floating in the sea but no bodies, either dead or alive.

"We cruised around the scene for an hour or two, then pursued our course south. The steamer Roanoke stood by the same as we did and I understood she picked up a body or two and one of the survivors."

One of the survivors of the Columbia gives this graphic description of the wreck:

"My God! How fortunate I am to survive this terrible disaster off the Mendocino coast. In allowing my mind to gather in the details of that terrible wreck my heart goes out to the relatives and friends of Capt. P. A. Doran, of the Columbia, and his conscientious and competent seamen. A hero in the face of terrible disaster, he went down to his grave with his ship after he had performed one of

OUTWARD BOUND FOR NOME, ALASKA
LEAVING DOCK AT SEATTLE, WASH.

HEADED FOR EL DORADO, Pacific Coast Steamship Company's **Senator** drops her lines from Seattle Pier at beginning of long voyage to Nome. Built at San Francisco in 1898, **Senator** was a typical coastwise liner of her era. Steel-hulled, of 2400 gross tons, she was 280 feet long, was propelled by an 1800-horsepower reciprocating steam engine.

STEAM SCHOON SAN PEDRO, left, stayed afloat after collision with liner **Columbia** off California coast (page 41), but her freeboard was limited.

The Seattle Daily Times.

CITY OFFICIAL PAPER

SIXTEEN PAGES.   SEATTLE, WASHINGTON SATURDAY MORNING, JAN. 4, 1902.   FIVE CENTS EVERYWHERE.

STEAMER WALLA WALLA SUNK BY AN UNKNOWN SAILING VESSEL—TWENTY-SEVEN PERSONS MISSING

Loss of coastwise liners like the **Walla Walla** was a frequent source of headlines for western newspapers in earlier days. **Walla Walla** sank quickly after collision with French sailing ship, which was only moderately damaged. (Page 40)

largely on the steamships for their transportation needs. Numerous independent lines, many of them one-ship companies, were formed to serve these secondary ports, but few of them flourished for long. They were in competition with the ubiquitous steam schooners, that breed of small wooden lumber carrier peculiar to the West Coast. These little craft poked their blunt noses into every port and doghole along the coast and most of them carried passengers, usually in doghouse-sized staterooms with three bunks piled one above the other. The steam schooners seldom sailed on precise schedules and honeymooning couples sometimes found a complete stranger occupying the "Aunt Mary," which was the steam schooner term for the top bunk in the three-level staterooms, but the fare was low and the food usually good.

Typical of the more successful independent small operators was the Oregon & Coast Steamship Company, organized to serve the smaller coastal towns. In 1888 the new company bought the Astoria-built *Emma Hume*, had her lengthened and renamed *Alliance*. With the little

coasters *General Miles*[3] and *Dolphin,* a schedule was maintained between Puget Sound, Portland and the fishing and lumber ports of Willapa Harbor and Grays Harbor. The Oregon & Coast line enjoyed a healthy trade until Jim Hill pushed a branch of his Northern Pacific Railroad west to the harbor towns. The combination of steam schooner and railroad competition put the line out of operation before the turn of the century.

As late as 1914, however, eleven companies were competing for the coastwise passenger and freight business, although the Pacific Coast Steamship Company was doing more business than the rest of them combined. It was the coming of highway and air competition after World War I that put the coastal liners in the boneyard.

3 The **General Miles,** built originally as a Coos Bay bar tug, was lengthened and converted to a freight and passenger steamer. She lived a long, hard life and will be heard of later as the pioneer vessel of the Alaska Steamship Company under a second name, **Willapa.** It was under a third name, **Bellingham,** that she was destroyed by fire in 1950 as a feature of Seattle's first Seafair.

SHIP OF MANY ADVENTURES was the **Umatilla**, saved from an uncharted reef off the Washington Coast in 1883 by Dynamite Johnny O'Brien (page 37), she suffered numerous lesser strandings, rammings and misadventures to serve under both Pacific Coast Steam and Admiral Line **houseflags**; was wrecked off the Japanese coast in March, 1918.

The old photograph below shows repair work under way on the **Umatilla** at Esquimault, British Columbia, following her narrow escape from complete disaster in 1883.

In the later years of Pacific Coast Steamship Company history it was H. F. Alexander's Pacific Alaska Navigation Company (with its subsidiary Pacific Navigation Company operating the *Yale* and *Harvard* south from San Francisco), plus two railroad-owned lines, the Great Northern Pacific Steamship Company and San Francisco and Portland Steamship Company, that gave Pacific Steam its major competition. The two-ship Great Northern Pacific line was operated by Hill's Great Northern and Northern Pacific Railway, the three-ship San Francisco and Portland line by Harriman's Union Pacific, which had gobbled up the old Oregon Railway and Navigation Company.

Dominant as it became, the Pacific Coast Steamship Company was unable, during its forty-year history, to make itself a monopoly. It remained for H. F. Alexander to organize the combined fleet which was to bring the coastwise steamship trade to its highest development and see it through its sudden decline and ultimate dissolution.

Since the Pacific Coast Steamship Company, during the four decades from 1877 to 1916, had

IN HAPPIER DAYS, passengers climbed the Valencia's rigging to have their picture taken as she loaded freight and passengers for Nome. A few years later terrified people lashed themselves in that same rigging in a futile effort to escape death as the steamer pounded to pieces on the west coast of Vancouver Island.
Below, Captain Westerlund on the bridge of the S.S. Alameda.

12th EXTRA

THE WRECKED STEAMSHIP VALENCIA

BAMFIELD—The Valencia has gone to pieces. All on board are lost.

VICTORIA, Wednesday, Jan. 24, 1:40 p. m.—The steamers Queen and Salvor were unable to find any survivors of the Valencia still on the wreck at 9 a. m. today It is supposed all are lost.

TRAGIC NEWS was told by newspaper extras headlining the Valencia disaster, above. Only a handfull of her company survived, shown on the opposite page battling the gray swells of the Pacific in lifeboats to reach the rescue ship City of Topeka. Some of them, showing the strain of their ordeal, are pictured at the bottom of the page, safe aboard the Topeka.

Left, Pomona worked Pacific Coast Steam's southern routes, was wrecked near Fort Ross, California in March, 1908.

more vessels in operation than the combined fleets of its competitors, it was inevitable that it should suffer a proportionate share of the marine disasters which were all too common during that period. Two of the vessels which were to be involved in particularly sensational shipwrecks were originally brought to the West Coast by the Oregon Improvement Company to transport coal between Puget Sound and San Francisco. They were the *Umatilla* and *Walla Walla*, iron propeller steamers of about two thousand tons built at Chester, Pennsylvania in 1881.

The *Umatilla* engaged in her most famous escapade in 1884, before coming under Pacific Coast Steam ownership. Steaming south with a cargo of coal, the *Umatilla* was hooting her way through a murky night of wind-whipped snow and sleet on February ninth. Off Cape Alava, most westerly point of the continental United States, the laboring collier crashed suddenly into an uncharted reef. Finding that water was rushing into the torn hull faster than the pumps could handle it, Captain Frank Worth ordered the ship abandoned. All the crew except First Mate Dynamite Johnny O'Brien and two sea-

SANTA ROSA, another victim of West Coast shipwreck, is shown above as she appeared in her younger days, before alterations included removal of one funnel. Her comparatively shallow draft made her well fitted for calls at San Pedro (Los Angeles harbor) which, fifty years ago, was plagued by a shallow entrance.

men got away safely in two boats. O'Brien and his two trusty shipmates went through the motions of abandoning ship via a small raft, but as soon as the captain's boat was out of sight they returned to the abandoned wreck.

As they scrambled up the steamer's iron sides, she worked loose from the reef and went drifting off broadside, pushed toward the graveyard coast of Vancouver Island by the wind and a strong northerly current. Dynamite Johnny and his crew of two set about raising enough sail to get steerage-way on the helpless steamship. Clawing away from the reef, the *Umatilla* was met by the northbound collier *Wellington,* which got a line aboard and began towing the sinking vessel toward the sheltered waters of Juan de Fuca Strait.

It was touch and go all the way, with the *Umatilla* down by the head and yawing like a stricken whale. Men of the *Wellington* were posted with axes to cut the towline when the *Umatilla* made her final plunge. The luck of Dynamite Johnny O'Brien, which was to become legendary on the Pacific coastal shipping lanes, did not desert him. The *Umatilla* made it all the way into the harbor of Esquimalt, British

Columbia. Then, with a vast, tired sigh of escaping air, she settled to the bottom of Equimalt's 40-foot deep harbor. Although out of service for a year, the *Umatilla* was eventually raised and put to work by Pacific Coast Steam, remaining on the California and Alaska runs of that line until taken over by H. F. Alexander's Pacific Steamship Company combine.

The uncharted reef upon which she crashed is now one of the best marked on the coast, for a red-hulled lightship rolls patiently there, her sides marked in great white letters . . . *Umatilla.*

The original *Umatilla* was to undergo many more misadventures during her long career, but none of them were fatal. In September, 1896 she found another uncharted reef, this time while crossing the Strait from Victoria for Port Townsend. This affair is a classic example of the happy-go-lucky manner in which maritime affairs were carried on in earlier days. Nobody aboard the *Umatilla* remembered that she was equipped with watertight doors so, although water was pouring into her from a thirty-foot hole in her bottom directly below the boiler room, the watertight doors weren't used. Although a thick fog blanketed the Strait, the keepers of the Race Rocks light on the Canadian side and Point Wilson light near Port Townsend hadn't bothered to start their fog horns blowing. They explained later that it had been a dry autumn with lots of fog, so there was no water in the fog horn boilers.

Thus plagued by inrushing tons of water and a complete lack of navigational help from shore, the *Umatilla* blundered ashore on Point Wilson within spitting distance of the lighthouse and its silent fog horn. Although at first given up as a total loss, she was again rescued and put back to work.

In 1903 she steamed into Seattle's Elliott Bay, started toward the Pacific Coast Company dock, then veered suddenly into the Northern Pacific dock, sailing majestically through it and ending up with her sturdy iron nose embedded in Railroad Avenue. Waterfront traffic de-

toured around her until she was extricated, practically undamaged and under her own power.

Later that year, an insane passenger became convinced that he was the skipper of the *Umatilla* and the only man aboard who could save her from distaster. Mounting to the bridge, he began issuing orders to the crew, much to the amazement of Captain Nopander, the steamer's real master. Eventually the captain decided to humor his deluded guest, who remained on the bridge all the way down the coast, periodically bellowing orders which he felt essential to the safe navigation of the ship. At San Francisco he politely turned the bridge over to Captain Nopander before being escorted ashore by several men in white coats.

In 1905, while shifting from the smelter to the coal bunkers in Tacoma, the *Umatilla* ran afoul of the lumber schooner *George E. Billings* during a heavy fog, smashing in a large section of the sailing vessel's hull. Two years later Captain Nopander suffered an experience as frustrating as that of the lunatic on the bridge. Another pea-soup fog enveloped the *Umatilla* in the Strait of Juan de Fuca and stayed with

ANGRY SEAS pound the little **Eureka** as she butts her way across the Humboldt bar.

her almost all the way to San Francisco. Captain Nopander had the steamer's whistle blasting at one minute intervals. Soon an answering whistle was heard, apparently close aboard. Thenceforth, whenever the *Umatilla* whistled, an answering blast came eerily out of the fog. When the fog finally thinned, no other ship was in sight and the mysterious whistle-blasts were heard no more, but while the passengers congregated at the rail searching for the mystery ship, a large whale came alongside and flooded them with a mighty spout from his blow-hole. It was an unusual voyage, even for the *Umatilla*.

The *Umatilla*'s sister-ship, *Walla Walla* had a more sinister career. After her coaling days, she was operated, along with the *Haytien Republic*[4] by the independent Merchants' Steam

4 Haytien Republic, in an effort to overcome her unsavory past, took the new name of Portland, the one under which she gained lasting fame as the treasure ship whose arrival in Seattle in 1897 started the Alaska gold rush.

Goliah, top, had early delusions of grandeur; tried to operate as coastal passenger ship in 1850's, later settled down to long career as San Francisco and Puget Sound tugboat. City of Puebla, lower, rests from her coastal journeying at Pacific Coast Company's Seattle pier below a skyline which, in 1899, boasted more trees than buildings.

ship Company of Portland in the San Francisco-Portland-Puget Sound trade. This firm was merely a front for one of the greatest smuggling operations ever undertaken in the United States. Stopping off at British Columbia ports, the *Walla Walla* and *Haytien Republic* would take aboard profitable but highly illegal loads of narcotics and Chinese emigrants bent on illegal entry into the United States. The smuggling ring involved shipping men, politicians and treasury agents, many of whom ended up wearing striped suits and reducing large rocks to small ones when the syndicate was finally broken up in 1893.

The *Walla Walla* was on the San Francisco-Puget Sound service of the Pacific Coast Steamship Company when, on the early morning of January 2, 1902, she steamed south toward the Golden Gate, the beam of the Cape Mendocino beacon clearly visible from her bridge. Ahead were the red and green running lights of a sailing ship, but there was plenty of searoom and no reason to change course.

Suddenly the pre-dawn darkness was shattered by staccato, urgent blasts of the *Walla Walla*'s whistle. The illusion of safety was gone and the sailing ship, a big bark, was looming close aboard. The blow, when the two ships came together, was a stunning one. As in the *Pacific* disaster, the windship, badly damaged, drifted off intent on her own survival, but it was the steamship which had received her death blow.

The ensuing minutes aboard the *Walla Walla* were described by her fourth officer, Cecil Brown:

"I never saw such a panic. Men and women were running about the decks wild with fright and it was almost impossible to get them to obey instructions. I have been in several shipwrecks, but I never saw people before who were so opposed to being saved."

Discipline was poor. Stokers from the engine room rushed the boats, pushing women and children aside and saving themselves. Lifeboats with half a dozen men aboard rowed past rafts and bits of wreckage to which scores of helpless people were clinging, making no attempt at rescue. The *Walla Walla* sank quickly and, had she not been right on the heavily travelled coastal shipping lane, the loss of life would have been terrible. It was bad enough as it was. Although the steamers *Dispatch* and *Nome City* were on hand picking up survivors by dawn, more than thirty victims went down with the old *Walla Walla*.

It was not until several days later that it was learned the French Cape Horn bark *Max* was the sailing vessel involved in the sinking of the *Walla Walla*. Although badly damaged, the *Max* made it safely to Puget Sound.

There was some muttering along the Pacific Coast waterfronts, for it seemed strange that the sailing ship should emerge with only moderate damage from an impact which swiftly sank the passenger steamship. The scattered questions became a roar of public indignation when, five years later, the Pacific Coast Company's liner *Columbia* went down off Shelter Cove.

The *Columbia* was a real oldster, for when she was built by John Roach back in 1879, she made history by having installed aboard the first Edison electric lighting system ever placed in a ship, Edison having perfected his invention that very year.[5] *Columbia* was considered a speedster in her day, for her single screw could drive her along at 14 knots, which was a fast pace in 1880; she was making close to her full speed as she steamed north from San Francisco toward Portland on the night of July 20, 1907. Aboard were 189 passengers and a crew of sixty. Eight bells struck; midnight and the change of watch. On the foc'sl Sven Peterson, A.B., took over the lookout's post, but it was pretty much a formality. Heavy fog blanketed the ship and he could barely make out the dim loom of bridge and pilot house. Forward there was only the gray-black void of foggy darkness muffling all sounds except the rush of water under the fast-moving steamer's bow.

Unheard and unseen, the little wooden steam schooner *San Pedro,* southbound from Grays Harbor, jogged along on a converging course with the *Columbia,* the distance between them closing fast. The steam schooner was less than a hundred yards away and almost dead ahead when Peterson saw the dim glow of her lights through the fog. His bellowed warning reached the bridge and steam spurted at the liner's stack in a series of short, desperate whistle blasts. The *San Pedro's* whistle shrieked a despairing encore to the *Columbia's* disaster signal as the

5 According to Capt. R. E. Cropley, Curator of the Seamans' Church Institute marine musem, "this pioneer generating plant is now in the Smithsonian Institute in Washington — such a small piece of machinery one wonders how on earth it did the job. And it's darn lucky the Smithsonian got it when the **Columbia** was modernized, for otherwise it would be at the bottom of the sea off California."

1

0ATTLE SUNDAY TIMES, FEB. 23, 1902.

PACIFIC COAST STEAMSHIP C
AFFORDS A COMPLETE COASTWISE SERVICE, COVERIN
Alaska, Washington, Oregon, California, Mex
SAILINGS FROM SEATTLE

Nome Route, Sailing 6 p. m.	**SENATOR**—June 1 / **STATE OF CALIFORNIA**—June
Southeastern Alaska Route Sailing 9 p. m. For Skaguay, Juneau, Ketchikan and Way Ports. As per schedule, connecting at Skaguay with trains of the White Pass & Yukon Railway Company for Dawson and interior points.	**CITY OF SEATTLE** — Feb. 2 March 12 / **AL-KI**—March 1, 15 / **CITY OF TOPEKA**—
Sitka Route Sailing 9 p. m. For Ketchikan, Juneau, Skagway (Sitka, southbound) and way ports.	**COTTAGE CITY**—March 1, 16
San Francisco Route Sailing 9 a. m. To San Francisco Calling at Port Townsend and Victoria Connecting at San Francisco with steamers for Southern California, Mexico, Australia, Honolulu & Orient	**QUEEN** — Feb. 23, March 10. / **UMATILLA**—Feb. 28, March 15 / **CITY OF PUEBLA**—March 5, 20
From San Francisco To Seattle, Tacoma, Port Townsend, Whatcom, Everett, Fairhaven, Anacortes, Vancouver and Victoria. Sailing from Broadway wharf 11 a. m.	**UMATILLA**—Feb. 21, March 7 / **CITY of PUEBLA**—Feb. 25, March / **QUEEN**—March 2, 17

All steamers carry both freight and passengers. Right to change steamers sailing dates is reserved.
SEATTLE OFFICES...... Ocean Dock, 113 James St. { SAN FRANCISCO OFFICES............ 10 Market Street. 4 New Montgomery

liner's high iron prow veered sharply toward, not away from, the little wooden lumber carrier.

The *Columbia* sank within eight minutes. The *San Pedro,* although almost awash and completely helpless, remained afloat. Almost one hundred men, women and children were drowned. The remainder were picked up by the *San Pedro* and the *George W. Elder,* or made it ashore along the Mendocino County coast in boats and rafts.

Feeling against the steamship company ran high all along the coast. San Francisco newspapers reported "Strewn along the rock-lined shores of Shelter Cove are bodies of children who were plunged to their death when the steamship *Columbia* dived, prow first, into the still waters of the Pacific. The faces of those children whose bodies have been recovered are for the most part peaceful, as the little ones knew no awakening when, still wrapped in slumber, they perished with the tremendous inrush of water as the ill-fated craft sank. They are no more of this earth, yet this fearful slaughter of the innocents cries out against corporate greed and the official red tape which denies protections to the thousands who trust their lives to the ancient craft now doing duty as passenger carriers on the Pacific."

41

ORDEAL BY FIRE was suffered by Pacific Coast Steam's proud new flagship **Congress** in 1916. Above, she's pictured with the fire raging uncontrolled and lifeboats being filled and lowered. Lower photos show the burned-out hulk under tow and undergoing later repairs which saw her eventually emerge as the Admiral Line's **Emma Alexander.**

In Seattle the newspapers bitterly front-paged reports like this: "The passenger ships of the Pacific Coast are with few exceptions so rotten that the least accident crushes them like eggshells and sends them to the bottom. The vessels used on this coast are the cast-offs from the East Coast, where they have been practically worn out and are sold for a song to the Pacific shipping companies. There are only six really safe passenger ships on the Pacific, four trans-Pacific liners belonging to the Pacific Mail Steamship Company, the *Minnesota* and the coastwise liner *President*. Most of the passenger ships on this coast are so old that one can throw a rivet hammer through them."[6]

The Pacific Coast Company's *Valencia*, not a new ship when the government used her as an Army transport during the Spanish-American war, had figured in an even worse tragedy only a little more than a year before the *Columbia* disaster. North-bound from San Francisco

6 Such criticism wasn't confined to the West. New York papers quoted Capt. William Norton of that city as follows: "The **Columbia** was one of the old single-screw steamers sent out to the Pacific Coast years ago. There were several John Roach shipyard boats that plied in eastern waters and were then sent around the Horn to California. The **Columbia** was built without modern water-tight compartments. She had old iron dividing doors, which I doubt very much would have worked in an emergency. **There are many other boats like her on the Pacific Coast.**

A RICH MAN'S TOY was probably the opinion of these pre-World War 1 San Pedro longshoremen as they trundled the shiny Detroit Electric aboard the steamer **Yale** to voyage, with its owners, to the opening of the San Francisco opera season.

... photo courtesy Jack Dillon

to Puget Sound, she blundered onto the rocks off Vancouver Island and was forced broadside against a sheer cliff too high to scale. While would-be rescue craft kept a helpless death-watch offshore, the *Valencia's* passengers lashed themselves in the rigging as the breakers quickly smashed the old iron hull to fragments. Only 27 escaped from the wreckage of the *Valcenia*, while 117 names were added to the death roll of the coastal liners. Among other minor irregularities, a subsequent investigation revealed that the *Valencia's* patent log was completely unreliable, making it almost impossible for her master to judge his position in a fog, and that she was equipped with tule-filled lifejackets, which were inexpensive, but had one undesirable feature . . . they wouldn't float.

There is little evidence, however, that the steamship company made any very determined effort to mend its ways. In 1911, five years before its long reign ended, its old iron steamer *Santa Rosa* hit the breach at Point Arguello. With relatively calm seas, the steam schooner *Centralia* was able to work in close to the stranded liner with the intention of taking off the passengers. Captain Farria of the *Santa Rosa*, in communication with his owners by wireless, was told to keep his passengers aboard

Alameda's dining salon was both neat and gaudy, in best tradition of nineteenth century marine architecture.

Social hall of **Jefferson** was typical of earlier coastal liners. Sign on center pillar prohibited gambling, a precaution against cardsharps who rode the steamers.

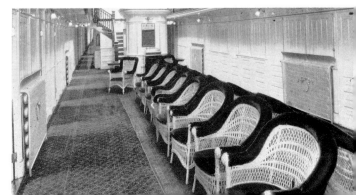

until the line's *President* came to take them off, as the steam schooner's owners would probably send in an exorbitant bill for their services, besides which, it would be expensive to transport the passengers overland to San Francisco!

The *Centralia* was sent on her way and when the wind rose to send the *Santa Rosa* smashing ashore, broken into two pieces, four lives were lost in the frenzied rescue efforts by lifeboat and raft.

During the *Santa Rosa's* final hours, ship's officers advised the frightened passengers against putting on the lifejackets provided for their safety. "They're filled with tule," it was explained, "and they won't float. We always buy our own cork jackets and keep them with us when we're working for Pacific Coast Steam."

Such were the Good Old Days aboard the Pacific Coastal Liners.

Much valuable material on the Pacific Coast Steamship Company and Admiral Line are contained in a monograph by Mr. H. B. Brittan, published in 1958, courtesy of Commander A. D. Yost, U.S.N.

MEN WHO MADE THEM GO were the engineers who nursed the sometimes cranky steam engines of the old-time coastal liners. Chief William Teideman of the **Jefferson** was one of them. (below)

RETIRED FROM COASTWISE passenger service, the old Pacific Coast Company steamer **Curacao** became the Greek freighter **Helenic Skipper**. On July 12, 1940, while plowing through heavy seas 125 miles off Grays Harbor, was wracked by a sudden explosion and fire which quickly terminated a career begun in 1895. The photographs above show her at dock in Aberdeen loading her final cargo of lumber and about to take her final plunge into the deep Pacific.

PACIFIC COAST STEAM

Left, top to bottom: **Orizaba** (1), 246-foot wooden side-wheeler, was built at New York in 1854, ran coastal routes from Puget Sound to Panama until scrapped in 1887. **Al Ki**, built Portland, Maine, 1884 and entered Alaska trade about 1896, passing to Northland S.S. Co. in 1910. Wrecked May, 1917, Point Augusta, Alaska. **Oregon** was brought west about 1886, passing to White Star line during gold rush days, remaining in Nome trade until September, 1906 when she was lost off Cape Hinchinbrook, Alaska.

Right, top to bottom: **Eureka,** known in early days as the **Little California**, began running to Alaska in 1866, served many routes and owners for nearly a generation. **Corona** was built at Philadelphia in 1888 to replace the wrecked **Ancon**, later served Coos Bay and Humboldt River ports. **Queen of the Pacific** as she appeared in her youth before her name was shortened. **State of California**, built in 1879, sank in Gambier Bay, Alaska, in August, 1913 with loss of 35 lives.

ADMIRAL LINE

Coastwise passenger steamship service grew up, came of age and then withered and died, all in the brief period between world wars. From 1914 to 1936 were the glory days of the coastal liners. The slow, uncomfortable and often decrepit old wooden and iron tubs gave way to fast, sleek steel steamers. Cramped and mouldy discomfort was replaced by spacious luxury, and the racing liners off the coast kept schedules equal to those of the express trains ashore.

To this generation of coastwise voyagers, the Admiral Liners were synonomous with sea travel between the ports of America's West Coast. From the beautiful turbine steamers *Yale* and *Harvard*, racing tirelessly between San Francisco and Los Angeles, to the *H. F. Alexander*, legendary "Galloping Ghost of the Pacific Coast" knifing between the Golden Gate and Puget Sound, and the Admiral boats of the Alaskan run, this steamship line literally covered the Pacific Coast.

The man who built the Admiral Line, Hubbard Foster Alexander, was born in Colorado Springs in 1879. As a child, he moved to Tacoma with his family and, by the time he was fourteen, he had a job on the Tacoma waterfront. Within six years he owned a controlling interest in the Commercial Dock Company and he had a canny eye peeled for other profitable maritime enterprises.

Late in 1905 a new steamship company made Tacoma its terminus. The Alaska-Pacific line, controlled by the Barneson-Hibbard company of San Francisco, had bought a pair of 1200-ton West Indies fruit steamers, the *Buckman* and *Watson*, with which they proposed to challenge the supremacy of the venerable Pacific Coast Steamship Company in the San Francisco-Puget Sound trade.

Alexander noted that the staunch little steamers made it around from the East Coast without undue trouble and soon proved themselves capable of maintaining a respectable, if not record-breaking schedule of eighty hours between San Francisco and the Sound. When in 1907, the Alaska-Pacific Steamship Company found itself in financial difficulties, young Alexander bought it. A few months later he acquired the Alaska Coast Company, which had been operating small passenger and freight steamers between Seattle and Alaskan ports since gold rush days.

At the age of 27, H. F. Alexander was president of a respectable shipping company. In addition to the steel liners *Buckman* and *Watson*, the new company operated the old Alaska Coast steamers *Portland*, *Jeanie* and *Bertha*. The newer ships were retained in the California trade, running between Puget Sound, San Francisco and San Pedro, while the smaller and older vessels continued to serve the northern routes.

Two of the old Alaska boats had earned their share of headlines before Alexander took them over. The *Portland*, of course, had gained lasting fame when, on the morning of July 17, 1897, she had steamed into Elliott Bay from Nome with the legendary "ton of gold" that started the Klondike stampede. The *Jeanie*, a sturdy steam schooner with a background of Arctic exploration and seal-hunting, had made tragic news when, in November, 1906, she rammed and sank the little Puget Sound passenger steamer *Dix* with a loss of 42 lives. In 1902 the *Portland* and *Jeanie*, Nome-bound, were caught in the Arctic ice off Cape Prince of Wales and posted

SPEED QUEENS OF THE PACIFIC, Admiral Liners **Emma Alexander** (ex-Congress) and **H. F. Alexander** (ex-Great Northern) at Pacific Steamship Company's Seattle piers. (Opposite page)

FIRST ALEXANDER SHIPS were the little ex-banana boats Buckman, above, and Watson,
Later renamed Admiral Evans and Admiral Watson, they formed nucleus of legendary Admiral Line. Lower, left to right, Alaska steamers Jeanie, Portland and Bertha were soon added to fleet when Alexander took control of the Alaska Coast Company. M. F. Plant, far right, added to fleet in 1911, had checkered and unlucky career under many names. As Yukon, struck reef off Sannak Island, Alaska in June, 1913 and became total loss.

Arctic steamer CORWIN ran spirited competition to Alexander steamers on northern sea routes

missing for 52 and 48 days respectively. They were given up for lost, the papers of June 28, 1902 somberly reporting that "there is not thought to be one chance in fifty" for the lost steamers to be saved. Eventually, however, they were discovered by the whaler *Belvedere*, after which they succeeded in making thir way safely to Nome.

The newer steamer *Buckman* soon figured in sensational news too. Murder and piracy on the high seas were stalking the West Coast sea lanes and, in late August of 1910, the humdrum little *Buckman* became the scene of startling violence.

The pirates of the *Buckman* came aboard innocently enough as paid passengers. One of them, French West, was a young man who had served in the U.S. Navy, attaining the rating of quartermaster. Later he attended Captain Marshall's nautical school on Colman Dock in Seattle, successfully passed the examination for a second mate's ticket and made several voyages as mate of the coastwise schooner *Echo*. His companion was a neurotic and shifty-eyed youth named George Washington Wise whose profession, until then, had been hanging around

SHIPPING MAGNATES H. F. Alexander and Robert Dollar, with Mrs. Dollar, are pictured at Admiral Line pier, above. Lower photo shows social hall on **Dorothy Alexander.** On the opposite page are views of passenger and freight loadings of **Queen,** top, **Admiral Rogers,** center left, and **President,** lower left. Top to bottom, **Yale** and **Dorothy Alexander** dining salon.

ADMIRAL LINES

Left, top to bottom: **Queen**, of 1882, in later years as Admiral liner. **H. F. Alexander**, 12,000-ton, turbine-driven flagship of the fleet. **Dorothy Alexander**, was originally Pacific Coast Company's **President**. Sold to Portuguese owners in 1946, renamed **Portugal**, scrapped, 1952 in Italy.

Right, top to bottom: **Emma Alexander** was originally **Congress**, returning to West Coast in 1923 after seven years service with China Mail Line as **Nanking**. Became British transport **Empire Woodlark**, 1940; sunk at sea with cargo of gas bombs, 1946. **Admiral Evans**, built in 1901 as **Buckman**, renamed 1914 and scrapped in 1937. **Admiral Watson**, built in 1902 as **Watson**. Scrapped in Japan, 1934. **Governor** was an oil-burner in her later years; had towering funnels reduced to size shown in this photograph, taken shortly before her loss in 1921.

PACIFIC STEAMSHIP COMPANY

Left, top to bottom: **Admiral Farragut**, built 1898 for American Mail S.S. Co., purchased in 1912 by Alexander and sold to Japanese scrapyard in 1934. **Admiral Fiske** was new name for old **Senator** (after 1922). Scrapped, Japan, 1934. **Admiral Peoples**, built 1918 as **Plainfield**. Bought from Baltimore & Carolina S.S. Co. as **Mary Weems**, 1927. Sold to Northland Transportation Co., 1934 and renamed **North Sea**. Stranded near Bella Coola, 1947. **Admiral Schley**, built 1898, purchased from American Mail S.S. Co., 1913. Scrapped by Japanese, 1934.

Right, top to bottom: **Admiral Dewey**, same history as **Schley**, above. **Admiral Sampson**, first of American Mail S.S. Co. steamers of 1898 purchased by Alexander (1909), first twin-screw oil-burner in Alaska trade. Rammed and sunk by CPR **Princess Victoria**, Puget Sound, August, 1914. **Admiral Goodrich**, built 1913 as Independent S.S. Co. **Aroline**. In Admiral Line service 1916-1923. Sold to National S.S. Co., renamed **Noyo**. Lost off Point Arena, June, 1935.

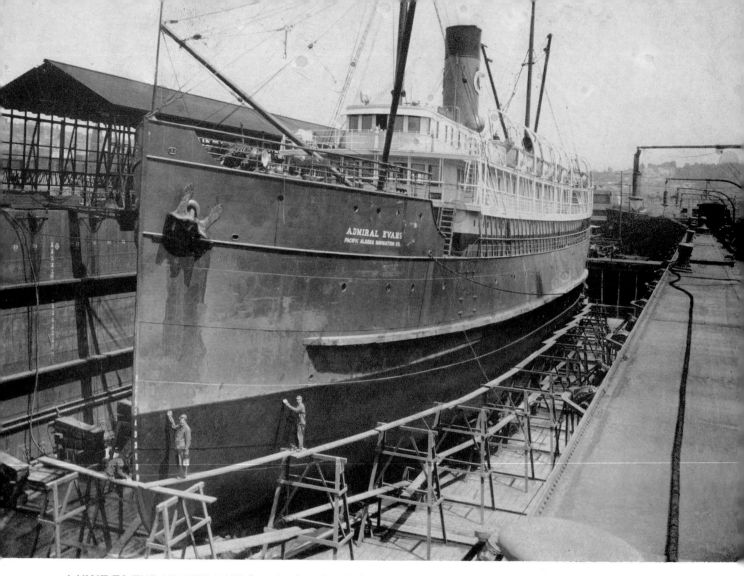

A VISIT TO THE BEAUTY SHOP for a hard-working lady of the sea, as the **Admiral Evans** has ravages of ocean voyaging removed in drydock. Painters working on red boot-top will work their way over green hull, white upperworks and buff and black funnel, with the **Evans** emerging in the bright and gleaming colors of H. F. Alexander's Pacific Alaska Navigation Company.

pool halls. Between them they had hatched a plot which would have done credit to the violent ward of an insane asylum.

Toward two o'clock on the morning of August 21, the *Buckman* was plodding quietly down the California coast. The night was dark, the sea calm, and Eureka lay somewhere off the port beam. It was a typical, routine sailing on the Puget Sound to San Francisco route. West and Wise prowled the deserted decks, the ex-mate carrying a shotgun; his partner a navy revolver. After a final whispered consultation amidships, West headed toward the cabin of the *Buckman's* master, Captain E. B. Wood. Wise moved stealthily toward the engine room. Their plan was forthright and simple. One would take charge of the bridge, the other the engine room.

Then they would drive the ship on the beach, loot the purser's safe, rob the passengers and escape to shore.

Captain Wood, at the age of 37, was a veteran of 24 years at sea. At the turn of the century he had been second mate on the *Roanoke* in the Nome trade. James McIntyre had been first mate and Captain Harry Weaver master. Captain Weaver had been stricken with pneumonia and died shortly after making port at Seattle. Mate McIntyre had died in the San Francisco earthquake. Superstitious sailormen said death usually came in threes at sea, but Captain Wood was a sober, level-headed man and his ship's business kept him too busy to worry about superstitions of the sea . . . until he opened his cabin door to face the leveled shotgun of the mad pirate, French West.

TYPICAL NORTHWEST HARBOR SCENE of World War 1 days is furnished by the veteran **Umatilla**, then in the last year of her long life, the then new steel lumber schooner **Redondo** in the stream and the tall masts of barkentine and schooner in the background.

The captain reached for his revolver and the blast of West's gun thundered through the sleeping ship. Captain Wood died instantly. As his slayer dashed toward the bridge a burly quartermaster, alerted by the sound of the shot, leaped at him from the darkness and wrested the gun from him. Cursing, West flung himself over the rail and into the darkness of the sea. The *Buckman* was twenty miles off shore and the murderer was not seen again. His partner, Wise, was overpowered by the engine room crew and placed in irons. Wireless messages informed owner Alexander and the authorities ashore of the tragedy aboard the *Buckman*. The liner *President,* headed north, swung off course to search for the killer who had gone overboard, but without success.

The surviving pirate, Wise, went violently insane during his trial. The *Buckman,* with a new master in command, went back to the respectable trade of shuttling passengers and freight up and down the coast, seldom making sensational news either under her original name, or the new one of *Admiral Evans,* which she was to assume in later years. Her third mate, John Thompson, did make something of a name for himself as human fog horn a year or so after the piracy episode, however.

Tacoma's harbor was blanketed with a pea-soup fog one November morning when the *Buckman* came groping up the Sound. The steamer's bow was invisible to the pilot on the bridge and it was going to be a problem to find the narrow entrance to the city waterway. Third

mate Thompson, who had developed a remarkable set of lungs through bellowing at seamen on coastal lumber schooners, hailed a Foss launch and departed for shore. His ensuing performance was recorded with considerable admiration by the waterfront editor of the Tacoma *Ledger*:

'He took his stand on the Commercial Dock, near the entrance to the waterway. The *Buckman* sounded an inquiring whistle. Thompson took a deep breath, opened his jaws and pierced the fog with a raucous imitation of a foghorn. The scheme worked like a charm. The *Buckman* answered his lion-throated roar and headed for the waterway. Thompson continued along the dock, keeping slightly ahead of the vessel. At intervals letting out a roar that reverberated across the intervening stretch of water. It was heard up town in the business section several blocks away. Every time the *Buckman* got slightly off her course in the waterway or felt uncertain, she blew her whistle and Thompson fog-horned back. The vessel reached the company dock without any trouble."

With such stout and resourceful men as mate Thompson running his ships, it is no wonder that H. F. Alexander prospered. A long step forward was taken when, in 1910, the Pacific Navigation Company, operating the fleet white sisters, *Yale* and *Harvard* between San Francisco and Los Angeles, became affiliated with the Alexander interests. The *Buckman* and *Watson* made San Francisco their southern terminus, where passengers transferred to the *Yale* and *Harvard* for the voyage on to Los Angeles and, later, San Diego.

Built for the New York-Boston express service, the white twins were driven by twin screws from 10,000-horsepower Parsons turbines fed steam by twelve single-ended boilers. Their accommodations matched their speed and power, bringing a new standard of luxury to the Pacific Coast.

This was a further challenge to the old Pacific Coast Steamship Company, which was then operating *Senator*, *President*, *Governor*, *Spokane*, *City of Seattle*, *City of Topeka*, *Umatilla* and *Curacao* on the same routes served by the Alexander ships. In 1913 the older line brought out the fine new two-stacker *Congress*, a move which was amply countered by Alexander. He bought and transferred from the East Coast the former United Fruit steamers *Admiral Sampson*, *Admiral Farragut*, *Admiral Dewey* and *Admiral Schley* between 1909 and 1914. That same year he merged the two original companies, the Alaska Coast Company and the Alaska-Pacific Company (Anchor Line), as the Pacific Alaska Navigation Company, taking, for the first time, the trade name Admiral Line. The *Watson* was renamed *Admiral Watson*, the *Buckman*, *Admiral Evans*.

By 1916 the pioneer Pacific Coast Steamship Company had definitely been put in second place. Hard-pressed not only by the aggressive Admiral Line, but by the San Francisco and Portland Steamship Company and the Great Northern Pacific Steamship Company's fleet and beautiful liners *Great Northern* and *Northern Pacific*, the Pacific Coast Company was not paying dividends acceptable to its eastern backers. As a crowning blow, its flagship *Congress* caught fire off Coos Bay. There was no loss of life, but the fire left the big steamer a burned-out shell.

In September, 1916, H. F. Alexander bought out the venerable Pacific Coast Steamship Company to form the new Pacific Steamship Company. A new house flag, combining the traditional red Maltese cross of the Pacific Coast Company and the white stars of the Admiral Line was hoisted on the 21 vessels of the combined fleet. Alexander had also purchased the *Aroline*, only steamer of the Independent Steamship Company, renaming her *Admiral Goodrich*. The only remaining competition was the San Francisco and Portland Steamship Company, controlled by the Harriman railroad interests and operating the big liners *Bear* and *Beaver* and the older *Rose City*, and the Great Northern Pacific Steamship Company with its splendid twins, *Northern Pacific* and *Great Northern*.

In the fall of 1916 the *Bear* grounded near the mouth of the Bear River in Mendocino County. Five lives were lost and the ship broke up. War shortages made it impossible to replace her. A year later the *Great Northern* and *Northern Pacific* were taken over by the government for war service. They were soon followed by the San Francisco and Portland liner *Beaver*, leaving only the *Rose City* in competition with the Admiral Line by the close of World War I.

The only major war losses of the Admiral Line were the *Yale* and *Harvard*, taken over by the government as English Channel transports. Both survived the war, but when, in 1920, they were made available for civilian purchase, a new company, the Los Angeles Steamship Company, outbid Alexander for them. This was a

serious blow to the Admiral Line, especially when, in 1921, the Harriman line chartered the Alaska Steamship Company's *Alaska* to run with the *Rose City* and made arrangements with the Los Angeles Steamship Company for an interchange of passengers and freight with the *Yale* and *Harvard* at San Francisco. However, the *Alaska* didn't last long on the California run. On August 6, 1921 she was steaming fast through the fog with 220 passengers aboard. She crashed onto the rocks at Blunt's Reef off Cape Mendocino and sank in a few minutes with the loss of 42 lives.

This was bad luck for coastwise shipping in general. The Admiral Line had lost its crack liner *Governor* in a collision off Port Townsend a few months earlier and public confidence in sea transportation was shaken. A crippling waterfront strike had tied up the West Coast ports, recession added gloom to the picture.

H. F. Alexander reacted aggressively. He chartered the twin-screw, 15-knot ex-German liner *Callao* and renamed her *Ruth Alexander*. The *President* was refurbished and renamed *Dorothy Alexander* to serve as running-mate to the *Ruth*.

In 1922 he added the finest ship of all to his fleet, the former *Great Northern*, which had gone to war as the *Columbia*. Renamed *H. F. Alexander*, she made her first run under the Admiral Line house flag on July 9, 1922. Two years later she received a general overhaul, including new boilers and propellers. After that she could knife through the ocean at twenty-five knots, gaining a place for herself as the all-time speed queen of the Pacific coastal fleet.

Another old rival was soon added to the fleet. The *Congress*, burned off Coos Bay back in 1916, had been rebuilt as the *Nanking* of the China Mail Line. Now she was bought by Alexander and renamed *Emma Alexander*. By 1923 the Admiral Line was making a million dollar profit, for the fast, luxurious new *Alexander* boats were enjoying a great vogue among travelers. Most of the older *Admiral* boats were engaged in slower schedule freight and passenger runs, or on the secondary Alaska route, among them the old *Senator*, renamed *Admiral Fiske*.

In 1927 the *Mary Weems* and *Esther Weems* of the Baltimore and Carolina Steamship Company were purchased and renamed *Admiral Peoples* and *Admiral Benson* respectively. These were the last passenger steamers acquired by the Admiral Line, although a number of war-

ADMIRAL LINES

Left, top to bottom: **Ruth Alexander**, veteran of two wars, was built in 1913 for North German Lloyd South American service as **Sierra Cordoba**; served as U-boat supply ship from secret bases in Straits of Magellan until interned by Peru and renamed **Callao**. Purchased and renamed in 1923. Taken over in 1939 by American President Lines and sunk by Japanese air attack off Netherlands East Indies, 1941. According to Capt. Kenneth Dodson, author of best-selling **Away All Boats**, who served aboard her, "The **Ruth** was the finest Admiral liner of them all." **Admiral Rogers** was the old **Spokane** with new name. **Admiral Rodman**, an eight-knot wooden steam schooner, was built in 1899 as the **Despatch.** Burned and scrapped at Seattle, 1937.

Right, top to bottom: **Iroquois**, East Coast liner, tried briefly to replace wrecked **Harvard** as running-mate for **Yale.** **Ravali**, wooden steam schooner built at Fairhaven, Cal. in 1905, burned and sank at Lowe Inlet, Alaska, 1918. **City of Seattle** in Admiral Line service.

ADMIRAL EVANS SAILS PLACID ALASKAN WATERS
on a 1921 voyage to southeastern Alaska ports, above.
ADMIRAL NICHOLSON, below, was a 678-ton steel steam
schooner built at Seattle in 1908 as the Northland (1) for
the Seattle-Ketchikan service of the Ketchikan Steamship
Co. (later Northland Steamship Co.). Sank in Alaskan
waters, 1916, was raised, sold to the Admiral Line and
renamed. Stranded near Umpqua River, Oregon, May, 1924.

built freighters were added to the fleet and operated for a short time.

By 1929 the big steamship company was in trouble. Savage rate wars had cut into profits and automobile travel was beginning to make itself felt. The great depression was the final blow. In 1931 H. F. Alexander resigned as president of the Admiral Line. Four years later the company was taken over by the Dollar Steamship Company and operated as a subsidiary of Dollar Lines until September, 1935, when passenger service ended. Freight service was suspended in January, 1936.

A Come-back try for the passenger trade was made by the *H. F. Alexander, Dorothy Alexander* and *Emma Alexander*, but it failed. The last Admiral Liner steamed from Puget Sound to San Francisco in September, 1936.

The Admiral Line was dead, and with it a way of life.

TYPICAL OF THE TWENTIES are high-wheeled Model-T's parked on the Seattle waterfront, with **H. F. Alexander** dwarfing the **Admiral Rogers** in the background, above, and the gay young voyagers who danced the Charleston in the **Dorothy Alexander's** ballroom, below.

H. F. BUMPS HER NOSE

When James J. Hill's crack coastal liner *Great Northern* went to war as the U.S. Transport *Columbia* she was the fastest ship flying the American ensign, carrying 72,000 troops between Hoboken and France in unconvoyed runs. After H. F. Alexander took her over, named her after himself and had her thoroughly overhauled, she was even faster. Her enormous turbines developed 25,000 shaft horsepower and she could do 27 knots when pushed; cruised easily at twenty-five. In 1915 she steamed from Honolulu to San Francisco in three days, 18 hours and 15 minutes . . . a record which stood for 40 years. Her regular schedule on the thousand mile run between San Francisco and Seattle was 39 hours. During her war service she frequently raced—and always beat—the giant liner *Leviathan.*

This speed, which earned her the nickname Galloping Ghost of the Pacific Coast, seldom got her into trouble, but on August 6, 1922 she failed to slow down to a cautious pace while running through a dense fog off the rugged Washington coast. She crashed head-on into Cake Rock, smashing her slim bows so badly that she suffered the humiliation of being towed

stern-first back to Seattle. Repairs cost almost a quarter of a million dollars.

WHITE SISTERS

Designed by William Denny & Bros. of Dumbarton and built by John B. Roach of Chester, Pennsylvania, *Yale* and *Harvard* were launched on December 1, 1906 and January 30, 1907, respectively. The handsome twins, 376 feet long and powered by 10,000-horsepower Parsons turbines, were built for the Cape Cod express passenger service of the Metropolitan Steamship Company of New York. Only one other American turbine steamer had been built before them. On their trials they made speeds of better than 24 knots.

When the financial activities of Metropolitan Steamship's guiding genius, Charles Wyman Morse, earned him a trip to a federal penitentiary in 1910, the rival New Haven Railroad exerted considerable pressure to have the two troublesome competitors *Yale* and *Harvard* removed from East Coast service. After passing through numerous corporate hands, they were chartered to the Pacific Navigation Company, an Alexander subsidiary, for San Francisco-Los Angeles service.

Sailing from New York on October 22, 1910, they made it to Los Angeles by way of the Straits of Magellan on December 16, where they established a four-trips-a-week scheduled between that port and San Francisco. In 1911 their southern terminus was extended to San Diego. The two handsome speedsters set a new standard of luxury for the Pacific Coast, maintained express train speeds and behaved themselves well in most weather, although heavy quartering seas had a tendency to make them stand on their heads when northbound in the winter.

In 1916 the *Yale* and *Harvard* were rechartered to the Pacific Alaska Navigation Company. Later in the year, when this line merged with the Pacific Coast Steamship Company their black funnels were repainted in the buff and black of the Admiral Line. Following their war service, during which they carried 368,777 troops between Southampton and Le Havre, they were taken over by the newly-formed Los Angeles Steamship Company for their old service. Their stacks were again painted black, the forward ones carrying two gold chevrons as testimonials of their war service.

The loss of *Harvard* in 1931 left *Yale* without a running mate for the next five years. In 1936 she was laid up and would doubtless have been scrapped had not a second world war extended her days. During the war she served as a dormitory for Puget Sound Bridge & Dredging Company and other construction firm employees at Sitka. Following a post-war period of inactivity in the reserve fleet at Olympia, the grand old lady of the California coast was towed away for scrapping.

SLEEK SISTERS Harvard and Yale, made San Francisco-Los Angeles trip a delightful experience until bad luck caught up with the **Harvard**, lower right, in 1931.

ONE EARLY MORNING in 1931 a rancher living on the hills above Point Arguello heard the melancholy cry of a steamship in distress. It reminded him of the *Santa Rosa* wreck which he had witnessed twenty years earlier, almost to the day, and at the same location. There was an uncanny similarity between the blasts of this ship's whistle and the voice of the long dead *Santa Rosa*.

Actually, he was hearing the *Santa Rosa's* whistle, for it had been salvaged and installed on the coastwise racer *Harvard* and the *Harvard*, on May 30, 1931, slammed ashore at 20 knots during her 972nd . . . and last . . . voyage between San Francisco and Los Angeles. Not one of her 490 passengers and crew of 60 was lost, but the beautiful *Harvard*, like the old *Santa Rosa*, was a total loss.

PACIFIC SHIPWRECK

When the Pacific Steamship Company's coastal workhorse *Admiral Benson* poked her nose into the sands of Peacock Spit on the evening of February 15, 1930 it looked at first like a minor stranding and, although the *Benson* became a total loss, no lives were lost. It was, however, one of the West Coast's more spectacular shipwrecks, since the steamer withstood the sea's pounding for a long time and her slow death was witnessed by thousands of visitors

from the high vantage point of Cape Disappointment, directly beneath which she lay.

The *Admiral Benson* was bound for Portland with 39 passengers, a crew of 65, and a cargo of fruit, groceries and assorted freight. The stranding took place near where the freighter *Laurel* had gone ashore and broken up a few months earlier and it seems probable that wreckage of the *Laurel* was mistaken for a channel buoy in the fog. The Columbia River bar was relatively calm, but the Coast Guard lifesaving crews from both sides of the river wasted no time in beginning the removal of passengers. The crew remained aboard, for there were high hopes of refloating the ship.

Three days after the stranding gale warnings were hoisted at the rivermouth Coast Guard stations and all the crew except Captain C. C. Graham were hauled ashore by breeches buoy. The ship's master stayed with her four more days, while mountainous seas, swept in by a forty-mile-an-hour gale, began the inevitable work of destruction. Finally, with the decks cracking and the hull filled with solid water, Captain Graham signalled that even he had given up hope. He was hauled safely to the

PACIFIC SHIPWRECKS VICTIMS were the Admiral Benson, shown on the opposite page shortly after she stranded on Peacock Spit, above, and as the ocean breakers began their work of destruction, below.
Admiral Liner Governor, above, met disaster off Port Townsend, Washington when she was rammed by the line's freighter West Hartland, shown with bow crumpled by collision in the lower photograph.

GOVERNOR FOUNDERS

RAMS BIG FREIGHTER AND SINKS

Admiral Liner Lost Off Point Wilson Near Port Townsend —All Passengers Rescued After Taking to Boats

ESCAPE IN LIFEBOATS

No Details Available; Vessel Was En Route to Puget Sound From San Pedro

SEATTLE, March 31.—The steamship Governor of the Admiral Line en route from San Pedro, Cal., to Seattle, rammed the freighter West Hartland, bound from Seattle to Bombay, and sank off Point Wilson, near Port Townsend, Wash., shortly before midnight, according to messages received by the port warden's wireless operator here.

A later report said all passengers were saved.

The first S O S received from the West Hartland at midnight said the Governor rammed the West Hartland and was sinking, the West Hartland escaping serious damage. It was reported the Princess Adelaide was en route and would arrive at the scene of the collision at 2:30 a. m.

At 12:55 a. m. another message from the West Hartland said: "No use sending Adelaide. Boat from West Hartland looking for survivors."

At 1:10 a. m. a third message from West Hartland said all passengers succeeded in escaping in lifeboats and had been picked up by West Hartland.

No details are available as to the cause of the collision. Officials of the Admiral Line here were notified, but were unable to give any further information.

The port warden radio office received another message from the West Hartland:

"Passengers all aboard accounted for. West Hartland due Seattle 4 a. m."

The collision, according to the port warden's office, occurred at the entrance to the Port Townsend harbor in a heavy fog. The steamers Princess Adelaide, Princess Alice and Jeptha were in the vicinity at the time.

Passenger List Lost

SAN FRANCISCO, Cal., April 1.—All passengers of the steamship Governor reported sunk off Point Wilson apparently were saved aboard the freighter West Hartland, which the Governor rammed prior to going down, according to radio advices received by the Chamber of Commerce here. The purser was brought aboard the freighter but had lost his passenger list, these advices stated.

The Governor, owned by the Pacific Steamship Company, had been plying along the Pacific Coast from Puget Sound to San Diego since she was built in 1907 in Camden, N. J. She was 391 feet long, 48 feet beam, of 5,474 gross tonnage and of 2,550 net tonnage.

She left here for Puget Sound March 29.

The Governor carried approximately 130 passengers when she left here, according to the manifest.

The Governor's crew approximated 26 men, most of whom were recruited in Seattle.

NEWSPAPER ACCOUNT OF WRECK, above, was overly optimistic in reporting no lives lost. A later count showed eight persons drowned.

beach along the Coast Guard lifeline and the *Admiral Benson* lay abandoned to the sea.

With no lives lost, the wreck of the *Admiral Benson*, while doubtless a blow to Mr. Alexander and the stockholders of the Pacific Steamship Company, brought prosperity to enterprising beachcombers, who retrieved items of cargo ranging from cases of lard to cases of fine watches, to beachfront hotels and restaurants which capitalized on the influx of shipwreck-attracted tourists, and to an enterprising female of easy virtue, who erected a tent on the beach, hung a red lantern from its ridgepole and dispensed sin on the sand to the lusty men of the salvage crew engaged in removing such items of value as could be reclaimed from the steamer's battered wreckage.

Although the Admiral Line placed in operation a far more seaworthy class of vessels than had its predecessors, it had its share of marine disasters, not all of them with the happy ending aspects of the *Benson* wreck. Some of them proved that even relatively modern steel ships could get into serious trouble, as had the burning of the Pacific Coast Company's fine new flagship *Congress* during the last year of that line's existence.

The wreck of the *Governor* was a case in point, for this big coastal liner, taken over with the Pacific Coast Company fleet, was a newer near-sister to the *President* which the Seattle newspapers had once classed as the only "safe" ship in the coastwise fleet. At the time of her demise she was only 14 years old. Built at Camden, New Jersey, she was registered at 5,474 gross tons; was 392 feet long. Her triple-expansion engines drove twin screws, giving her a speed of 16 knots. In 1913 she made the voyage from San Francisco to Seattle in 49 hours, which was a new record for that time.

She would not be considered a luxury liner by present-day standards, for in her day it was assumed that passengers could go fifty hours or so without taking a bath; consequently she didn't boast a single stateroom with private bath, nor did she have hot and cold running water in every room. Until her later years she belched coal smoke from twin funnels of gigantic proportions, described by one critic as "a pair of outrageous-looking pipe-stems that reared to the heavens above her decks."

After she was converted to oil fuel her soaring smokestacks were cut down, giving her a somewhat more streamlined and less top-heavy look. In 1921 she was considered a crack liner of the Admiral Line's Puget Sound to San Francisco shuttle. She was described as being "in her arrangements and finishing designed to secure the utmost comfort both for crew and passengers; her wide alleyways and shade decks afford excellent and ample space for promenading, and her social hall and smoking room are large, well lighted and handsome. A grand piano, supply of music and well-chosen library of 200 volumes are in the social hall for the use of passengers. By means of the Massie wireless telegraph system, passengers may communicate with the shore at any hour of the day and night. All the modern devices for decreasing the dangers of sea travel have been fitted, which, with her complete subdivision into water-tight compartments and her large size, makes the *Gover-*

HIGH AND DRY ON THE ALASKA COAST, the little Admiral Rodman, above, looks in a bad way, but she was safely floated on the next high tide.

The Portland-San Francisco steamer Rose City was bucking heavy seas on the Columbia River bar when this picture was taken from her hurricane deck in 1924, lower left. A couple of heavy seas came aboard to damage cargo and injure several crew members shortly after the photo was made. A year later, she presents a more gala appearance, lower right, as she lies at her San Francisco pier with flags flying in honor of the diamond jubilee of the Republic of California.   ... Courtesy Herbert Tiesler

nor one of the safest and most comfortable steamships yet put on the Pacific coastwise trade."[1]

Three years after her arrival on the coast, the *Governor* was headed north out of San Francisco, properly minding her own business, when the rival San Francisco and Portland Steamship Company liner *Beaver* came bustling out of a light mist off Cape Mendocino, headed in the same direction. As usual, in her coal-burning days, the *Governor* was busily belching awesome clouds of black smoke from her two skyscraper funnels and the *Beaver's* chief engineer dispatched a sarcastic radio message to chief Ben Maitland of the *Governor* inquiring whether the kind of coal they burned always acted that way, or were they incinerating galley garbage in the furnaces?

Outraged, Maitland sent a reply crackling back to the effect that the *Governor* could burn Irish peat and still beat the hell out of the oil-burning *Beaver*. Thus challenged, the *Beaver* did considerable smoking on her own account as the oil was poured to her fires and she came fussing and fuming up astern of the *Governor*. As the two liners sped past Eureka, Trinidad Head, Cone Rock and The Turtles, the *Beaver* slowly narrowed the gap. Another radiogram was delivered to chief Maitland: "Is that the best you can do?"

"Tell that misguided donkey-engineer we're doing sixteen and a half knots," Maitland roared at the radio operator, "and any minute now I'm going to stop fooling around and show him twenty knots!" Then he cast an imploring look at the bridge, where Captain Jepson, the *Governor's* master, was calmly watching the *Beaver* overhaul his ship.

By this time the *Beaver* was so close that the jeers of her passengers and crew could be heard aboard the *Governor*. Captain Jepson leaned over the bridge dodger. "Let her out and stop this nonsense," he told his chief engineer.

"Yes, *sir!*" Ben Maitland replied happily and dove for the engine room companionway. Minutes later the throb of the big reciprocating engines rose to a new, exciting tempo as the *Governor's* two hundred passengers headed aft to watch a broad gap suddenly widen between their ship and the straining *Beaver*.

"The *Beaver's* going backward!" a woman passenger shouted as the big Pacific Coast Company liner sped on toward Dragon's Rock and

1 Tacoma Daily Ledger, September 30, 1907.

IT WAS ACCIDENTAL when, in 1915, the **Admiral Watson** was rammed and sunk in Seattle harbor by the Pacific Coast Steamship Company's freighter **Paraiso**, top, opposite page, and when the **Admiral Evans** submerged temporarily at Hawk Inlet, Alaska, but the old **Admiral Rogers** was deliberately run ashore on a Puget Sound beach, opposite, lower and above, when plans were made to convert her to **a tourist hotel**. Things didn't work out, however, and in 1948 she was scrapped at Seattle.

Point Ferrelo while her erstwhile rival diminished to a smoky speck on the horizon and finally sank from view in the foaming wake of the racing *Governor*.

The *Governor* wasn't hurrying on the night of March 31, 1921. She had landed some of her north-bound passengers at Victoria and was making a leisurely run up the Strait toward Seattle. As midnight passed and the first day of April began, the pilot in the darkened wheelhouse picked up the bright gleam of Point Wilson light, at the entrance to Port Townsend Bay, and the dimmer glow of the Marrowstone Island beacon ahead. Soon thereafter he saw the range lights of a freighter gliding out of Port Townsend harbor ahead and to the right.

The freighter had the right of way, but there was plenty of room in the broad strait and no reason for alarm. Then, in the wink of an eye, there was no more room and no more time. The red port light of the freighter was gleaming balefully, close alongside and her whistle was blasting the frightening staccato of the collision warning. Then the steel prow of the *West Hartland* crashed sickeningly into the *Governor's* starboard side.

The *West Hartland*, under charter to the *Governor's* owners, the Pacific Steamship Company, kept her bow wedged deep in the passenger liner's side, enabling many of the *Governor's* people to clamber directly aboard, while temporarily plugging the gapping hole in the

Super Ship "H. F. Alexander," the world's largest, fastest and smartest coastwise liner. She is 525 feet long and provides every modern comfort, including a delightful Colonial Nite Club.

3 IN 1 SERVIC[E]

YOUR
1
TICKET } INCLUDES { 1 – TRA
2 – BE
3 – ME

Hotel-like STATEROOMS

Note the completeness of the facilities in these rooms, which might be likened to a miniature hotel room. Staterooms vary as to size, arrangement and location, but all embody the same features of comfort and service. The berths, or beds, are not portable affairs, but are built especially for sleep. They are generous in size, and are provided with restful springs and mattresses of modern type. A bed, or reading, light is conveniently arranged at the head of each berth. In your stateroom you dress and undress normally and there are closets or hangers where your clothes may be hung without annoyance to you—or effect on their appearance.

Keys are provided for each room and you come and go in much the same manner as you would use a hotel room. Its facilities are constantly available to you both day and night. You retire when you desire and get up when you please. Your toilet is made in its privacy, and its seclusion is yours at any time you desire freedom from intrusion.

Comfortable TRAVEL

When you travel-by-water you live comfortably. Each stateroom, regardless of type, provides ample space to dress and undress normally. Your toilet accessories are set out where they are constantly accessible and your toilet need not be hurried by the consideration of others.

Home-like FACILITIES

Women, particularly, appreciate the opportunity to keep up their appearance while traveling. You rarely see a weary or withered looking traveler on a steamship, for there is every opportunity to keep fresh and smart. First the roomy stateroom permits of the proper care of clothes and accessories and then there are the proper boudoir conveniences even down to an electric plug for curling irons. No wonder so many women prefer to travel by water!

Cocktail BARS

Each "Alexander" liner has an attractive Cocktail Bar where those accustomed to an appetizer before dinner, or a cordial after dinner, may enjoy their favorite concoction at shore prices. A wide choice of dinner wines and liquors is available in the dining saloon to add zest to your meals.

TYPICAL *Dining* SALOON

Three times a day the ship's family assembles enthusiastically in the dining saloon, where appetites made keen by salt sea air are quickly appeased by famously-good Admiral Line meals. You eat leisurely and comfortably, for the rooms are large, airy and inviting. Some idea of the size may be gained from the fact that the Colonial Dining Room on the "H. F. Alexander" seats 270 persons, while those of other steamships are proportionately as large. The table arrangement permits of individual groups of two, three, four or six persons.

VICTORIA

OAKLA[ND]
SAN FR[ANCISCO]

LO[S]

SAN DIEG[O]

THE ADMIRAL LINE
P.S.S.L.

The ADMIRAL LINE [PACIFIC STEAMSHIP LINES]

The "Emma Alexander" is a former trans-Pacific liner, 442 feet long, and is one of three Alexander liners which afford unusual coastwise service.

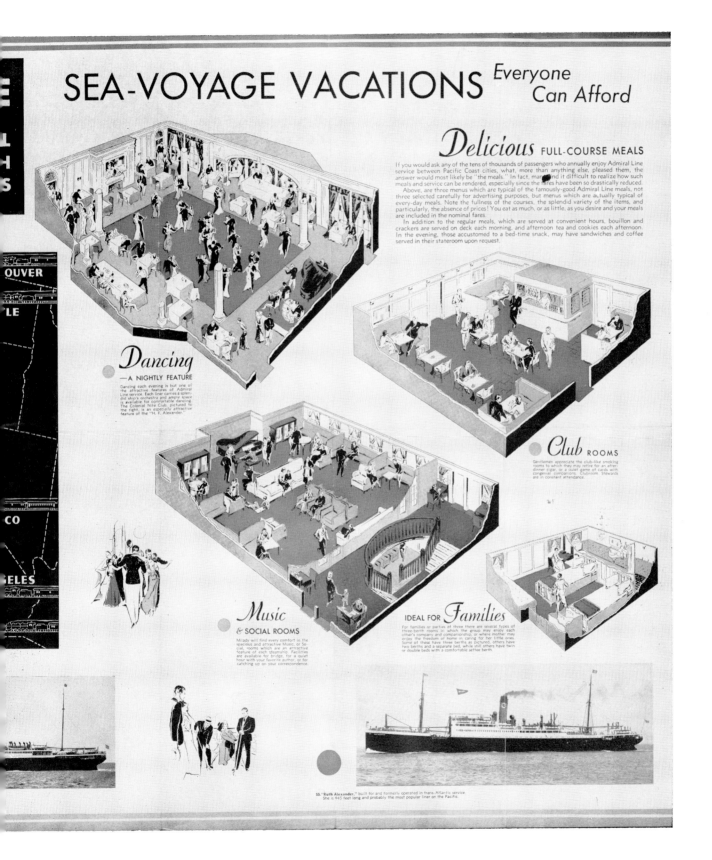

SEA-VOYAGE VACATIONS Everyone Can Afford

Delicious FULL-COURSE MEALS

If you would ask any of the tens of thousands of passengers who annually enjoy Admiral Line service between Pacific Coast cities, what, more than anything else, pleased them, the answer would most likely be "the meals." In fact, many find it difficult to realize how such meals and service can be rendered, especially since the fares have been so drastically reduced.

Above, are three menus which are typical of the famously-good Admiral Line meals, not three selected carefully for advertising purposes, but menus which are actually typical of every-day meals. Note the fullness of the courses, the splendid variety of the items, and particularly, the absence of prices! You eat as much, or as little, as you desire and your meals are included in the nominal fares.

In addition to the regular meals, which are served at convenient hours, bouillon and crackers are served on deck each morning, and afternoon tea and cookies each afternoon. In the evening, those accustomed to a bed-time snack, may have sandwiches and coffee served in their stateroom upon request.

Dancing
—A NIGHTLY FEATURE

Dancing each evening is but one of the attractive features of Admiral Line service. Each liner carries a splendid ship's orchestra and ample space is available for comfortable dancing. The Colonial Nite Club, pictured to the right, is an especially attractive feature of the "H. F. Alexander."

Club ROOMS

Gentlemen appreciate the club-like smoking rooms to which they may retire for an after-dinner cigar, or a quiet game of cards with congenial companions. Clubroom Stewards are in constant attendance.

Music
& SOCIAL ROOMS

Milady will find every comfort in the spacious and attractive Music, or Social, rooms which are an attractive feature of each steamship. Facilities are available for bridge, for a quiet hour with your favorite author, or for catching up on your correspondence.

IDEAL FOR Families

For families or parties of three there are several types of three-berth rooms in which the group may enjoy each other's company and companionship, or where mother may enjoy the freedom of home in caring for her little ones. Some of these have three berths as pictured, others have two berths and a separate bed, while still others have twin or double beds with a comfortable settee berth.

SS. "Ruth Alexander," built for and formerly operated in trans-Atlantic service. She is 445 feet long and probably the most popular liner on the Pacific.

liner's hull. Others were transferred to the *West Hartland* by lifeboat.

But, just as in the *Andrea Doria-Stockholm* disaster of 35 years later, some were trapped in their staterooms below decks. Two small girls, daughters of Mr. and Mrs. W. W. Washburn, were trapped in the wreckage of their berths and their mother stayed with them as the *Governor* rolled over, broke in two and plunged beneath the dark waters of Juan de Fuca's Strait. In all, seven passengers and three crew members went down with the shattered *Governor* on that dark morning off Port Townsend Bay.[2]

H. F. Alexander had long since learned that modern steamship design was not an absolute safeguard against disaster. The *Admiral Sampson*, first of his *Admiral* boats, was considered a fine craft, being noted as the first twin-screw, oil-burning steamship to ply between Puget Sound and Alaskan ports. Upon her arrival on the coast in 1909, she operated with the *Buckman* and *Watson* to institute sailings every five days between Puget Sound and San Francisco; every two weeks to Los Angeles. In 1912 she was completely overhauled and placed in the southwestern Alaska trade.

On August 26, 1914 the *Admiral Sampson* was hooting her way down Puget Sound through a dense pall of fog and darkness on what was expected to be another routine Alaska sailing. Off Point No Point the *Admiral Sampson* met the graceful three-stacker *Princess Victoria*, crack racing packet of the Canadian Pacific coastal fleet. She too was going it blind . . . and fast.

The two ships came together hard, the knife-sharp steel bow of the *Princess Victoria* slashing deep into the hull of the Admiral liner. The crews of both vessels responded ably to the emergency. The captain of the Canadian liner kept his ship's bow pressed into the rent in the American ship's hull, the engines moving slow

LIKE A CARVING KNIFE ON EDGE were the hull lines of the H. F. Alexander, pictured here in an East Coast drydock in her last years as the transport General George S. Simonds.

. . . Courtesy of Clarence N. Rogers

ahead, but the impact had started a fire in the *Sampson's* fuel tanks and flames were licking around the *Princess Victoria's* bow. Swift as the work of rescue was, the *Sampson's* final plunge was even swifter, for within fifteen minutes of the impact, the *Victoria* was forced to draw away; the first of the Admiral liners had found a final resting place in the deep waters of the Sound, sixteen of her passengers and crew dying with her[3], her master, Captain Zim

---

[2] Although there was no doubt that the **Governor**, having the **West Hartland** to starboard, was required by maritime law to keep out of the freighter's way, the reason for the disaster has always remained something of a mystery. The captains involved were among the most experienced in the Admiral Line service. Captain E. P. Bartlett of the **Governor**, a graduate of the New York nautical schoolship **St. Mary**, was the first master employed by H. F. Alexander when he brought out the first Admiral liners from the East Coast and was for some time master of the **Yale** on the San Francisco-Los Angeles route.

Captain John Alwen of the **West Hartland** was a veteran of a quarter century in the coastwise and transPacific service and, although he was in command of the old **Umatilla** when she was lost off the Japanese coast, he was fully exonerated from any blame in connection with that accident.

[3] This was the first loss of an Alexander-owned ship in which loss of life was involved, although the steamers **Portland**, **Jeanie** and **Yukon** had previously been wrecked in Alaskan waters and the East Coast steamer **Kentucky** foundered in the Atlantic while en route to the West Coast for Pacific Alaska Navigation Company service.

PRINCESS VICTORIA RAMS ALASKA SHIP IN FOG ON SOUND

Three passengers and eight members of the crew of the steamship Admiral Sampson are known to be dead and five others are reported as missing and probably drowned as the result of a collision at 6 o'clock this morning off Point-No-Point in which the C. P. R. liner Princess Victoria rammed the Admiral Sampson, of the Admiral line, and sent her to the bottom in four minutes after the crash.

Capt. Z. M. Moore, Chief Engineer A. J. Noon and W. E. Recker, first wireless operator, went down with the Sampson while trying to launch the last lifeboat after seeing the passengers removed from the sinking craft.

With them went Miss M. Campbell, stewardess; A. Sater, watchman; L. Cabaranas, third cook; C. M. Marquist, able bodied seaman, and J. C. Williams, a mess boy.

Those of the passengers known to be lost are:
MRS. GEORGE BANBERRY, wife of the Pacific-Alaska Navigation Company's agent at Skagway.
EZRA BYRNE, Seattle.
C. W. BRYANT, Seattle.

That this list does not cover the total of dead is the declaration of survivors and of the crews of both vessels who name five other persons, W. Hoffem, J. H. Cline, William Klovitch, John McLaughlin and one second-class passenger, a foreigner, as among the missing.

The survivors, both passengers and crew, were picked up by the Princess Victoria and returned to Seattle, arriving at the pier at 10:50 o'clock this morning. P. A. Obert, mate and pilot, was removed to Providence Hospital in a seriously injured condition, but will live. Ezra Byrne, after suffering terribly from burns sustained when he was caught in the wreckage and pinned in an inferno of flame, expired just as the Victoria docked.

SUNKEN STEAMER, SHIP THAT RAMMED HER, AND MAP SHOWING PLACE WHERE TWO CRASHED IN THE FOG

The top picture shows the ill-fated steamer Admiral Sampson, of the Admiral line, the photograph having been taken by a member of The Ledger staff on the recent "billion-dollar" excursion to Alaska. The picture in the center shows the Princess Victoria, whose prow sent the Admiral Sampson to the bottom. In the map below the star indicates Point-no-Point, where the disastrous accident took place.

LOW FOG AND HIGH SPEED were blamed for 1914 collision between Alaska cruise liner Admiral Sampson and Canadian Pacific express packet Princess Victoria. The Admiral liner sank within minutes of the impact. Captain Zim Moore was one of the dozen passengers and crew members who went down with the Admiral Sampson in mist-shrouded waters off Point No Point in Puget Sound.

Admiral Sampson in Alaskan waters, below.

Moore, chief engineer Allen J. Noon, radio operator W. E. Recker and stewardess M. Campbell, among them.

In the best tradition of the sea, the chief engineer and stewardess were attempting to save passengers trapped in their staterooms when the liner went down. Radio operator Recker was still at his set transmitting the dying ship's S.O.S., and Captain Moore was on the bridge, directing the rescue operations.

The steamships which competed with the Alexander liners in the last decades of the coastwise passenger ship era were not immune to mishap either. Most of them had their share of trouble, including Harriman's San Francisco and Portland Steamship Company, which was the new designation for the old Oregon Railway & Navigation Company.[4]

4 The San Francisco **Chronicle**, on August 26, 1904 reported, "Within another month the Oregon Railroad & Navigation Company's steamers between this city and Portland will be running independent of the railroad, although the line will continue as one of E. H. Harriman's interests. To relieve the railway of its Ocean Division, the San Francisco & Portland Steamship Company has been incorporated."

OPPOSITION BOATS on the coastwise routes included the **St. Croix**, brought to the West Coast for the Nome trade in 1909 by Schubach & Hamilton of Seattle. At the close of the season she engaged in a rate war with the Pacific Coast Company for San Francisco-Los Angeles business, remaining until November 20, 1911 when she was completely destroyed by fire off Santa Monica. No lives were lost.
BELFAST-BUILT as the **Mississippi**, in 1890, the U.S. Army Transport **Buford** had a brief career as an Alaska steamer when, in 1923, Fred Linderman of San Francisco dispatched her north under command of aging (73) Dynamite Johnny O'Brien. After co-starring with O'Brien and Buster Keaton in a motion picture (Page 78), the **Buford** went to Japan for scrapping in 1929.
Below, **Great Northern** of Hill's Portland-San Francisco line emerged from World War 1 service as **H. F. Alexander**.

NO STRANGER to reefs and shoals, the **Admiral Watson** is shown above following 1910 stranding on Waadah Island, Puget Sound.   . . . Courtesy G. R. Dennis

Northern Pacific, below, was running mate of **Great Northern** from 1915 until the two were taken over for World War 1 service. They beat the express trains by three hours between San Francisco and Portland.

On the night of June 14, 1916, one of its two newest and largest steamers, the *Bear*, strayed from her course amid the deadly maze of rocks and reefs off Cape Mendocino. Her master, veteran Captain Louis Nopander, who had coped with the madman on the bridge of the *Umatilla* back in 1903, was certain that his ship was several miles at sea up to the very moment that she crashed into a submerged reef a hundred yards off the beach. Even then the ship's officers were unsure of their position, for a heavy fog blotted out everything within a few yards of their stricken vessel. Considerable confusion resulted, with one lifeboat attempting to reach shore through the breakers. It capsized and five lives were lost. The other boats made it safely offshore to *Blunts Reef* lightship, guided by the lusty bellow of the lightship's fog horn. The 150 survivors passed a safe but very crowded night jammed aboard the lightship which had accommodations for a crew of ten. In the morning they were transferred to the steamer *Grace Dollar*, while the 29 half-frozen survivors of the capsized lifeboat were picked up from the beach and transported to the old Country Hotel at Capetown to be thawed out. Efforts to salvage the *Bear* failed and she became a total loss.

OPPOSITION BOAT Cuba had short-lived career on California-Puget Sound route for one-ship company; stranded on San Miguel Island on September 9, 1923.

Alameda, above, survived this 1905 stranding on the California coast to serve for decades as an Alaska liner.

Bear, above, was fleet-mate of Rose City, shown below, left, passing under Willamette River bridge at Portland and, right, at San Francisco pier, in Harriman-controlled Columbia River-Golden Gate steamship service which competed with Admiral Line.

MILLION DOLLAR SHIPWRECK of Harriman's crack San Francisco-Portland liner **Bear** on rocky Cape Mendocino shore cost five lives. All efforts to salvage the big steamer failed. Sister ship **Beaver**, lower left, survived to become World War 2 transport, lower right. Another wartime transport, **H. F. Alexander**, is shown in the center picture making her last voyage, in 1946, to the shipbreaker's yard in Philadelphia.

BAD LUCK FOR A LUCKY SHIP

The Pacific Coast Company's *Corona* was known as a lucky ship, for since her launching in 1888 she had suffered only one serious mishap and providence seemed on her side in that one. In 1898, while engaged in the Alaska gold rush traffic, she piled up on the rocks off Lewis Island. Although she was backed off, water was spouting through a gaping wound in her bow at such a rate that pumps and collision mats proved ineffective. Just as the abandon ship order was about to be given, the rush of water suddenly stopped. A thorough investigation revealed the source of the seeming miracle. A large blackfish had been sucked into the hole with such force that it jammed it completely. The fish had to be cut out with axes after the *Corona* went into drydock.

By March of 1907 the *Corona's* luck must have run out, for as she steamed across the Humboldt bar, inbound for Eureka, she veered suddenly from her course to pile up on the jetty in a welter of breaking seas. One lifeboat was lowered, immediately capsized with the loss of one life. After that the survivors waited for the Humboldt lifesaving crew, which duly arrived to perform a magnificent rescue operation be-

fore an audience of thousands which had gathered on the beach at the news of the steamer's loss.

A recent shifting of the sands at the Humboldt's mouth has exhumed one of the *Corona's* masts, still standing after more than a half a century . . . a mute reminder of the days when shipwreck was an accepted hazard of life on the Pacific Coast.

Columbia, ex-President, ex-Dorothy Alexander, came away with cuts and bruises after a spectacular collision with sister-Alaska Steamship liner Yukon.

Next Page: Captain Dynamite Johnny O'Brien, Buster Keaton and S.S. Buford star in silent film comedy, The Navigator.

GOLD RUSH

The Panic of 1893 had drifted westward the way a tule fog rises up in the marshes of the Sacramento and San Joaquin, drifts down the bay and out the Golden Gate and, in the words of Peter B. Kyne's immortal Captain Scraggs, "Just naturally blocks the wheels of commerce while she lasts." By 1897 there wasn't even the excitement of a panic to buoy up men's souls. There was only the drab montony of a depression.

Idle ships and idle seamen rotted on the backwaters of every West Coast port, going nowhere, waiting with growing hopelessness for the coming of better times.

In the Skidroad districts of Seattle, Portland and San Francisco, out-of-work sailors mingled with out-of-work loggers, miners and farm workers, providing poor kickings for the boxhouses, dives and gambling dens. Times were hard for pickpockets and prostitutes as well as sailors. Merchants contemplated shelves and warehouses loaded with unsold goods or threw up their hands and sank into bankruptcy. Even the Port Townsend crimps were doing badly, for shipmasters had plenty of hungry men to pick from and the blood money rate for human bodies delivered aboard the offshore windjammers had fallen to a new low.

Even the optimists were looking only a for a slow, gradual recovery, so everyone was surprised as well as delighted when the depression ended quite suddenly with a whoop and a roar and a vision of dazzling brilliance on the seventeenth day of July, 1897.

The roar was the throaty whistle-blast of the North American Trading and Transportation Company's Alaska steamer *Portland,* easing in toward Schwabacher's Wharf on the Seattle waterfront. The whooping emanated from the whiskery lips of a number of seedy-looking in-dividuals on her decks. The shining radiance was in the remarkably heavy baggage they lovingly tended . . . Bull Durham bags as heavy as sash-weights and foot-long moosehide pokes that made a strong man grunt to lift them.

The *Portland's* cargo was dramatic enough in its own right . . . a million dollars in pure gold! In the broader sense the *Portland's* arrival was of even greater significance, for she was bringing something the Pacific Coast had been waitin a long time for. *Prosperity!*

The *Portland* came very near being two days late winning a place in history for herself. The *Excelsior* had picked up the first of the Klondike miners at Nome and arrived at San Francisco on July 15 carrying almost as rich a treasure at the *Portland.* It was a publicity man named Erastus Brainerd who made the steamer *Portland* famous, gave the great gold rush to Seattle and made Alaska a "suburb" of that enterprising Pacific Northwest city. ....

Brainerd did it by coining a phrase which kindled the imagination of the world. Even in 1897 newspaper readers were innured to tales of millions, but who had ever heard of anything as splendid as the headline which emanated from Erastus Brainerd's publicity office at the Seattle Chamber of Commerce? *A Ton of Gold!*

A Ton of Gold at Seattle! The headlines blossomed in depression-ridden cities across the nation. This was romance and excitement and sudden high hope. The ton of gold had come to Seattle and that was the sensible place for a man to go looking for his personal share of the "New Eldorado," as the papers were calling the Klondike diggings. A motley horde of treasure-seekers converged on Seattle, spurred on by new barrages of inspired publicity from the agile brain and pen of Erastus Brainerd.

Having arrived at Seattle, the newcomers

GOLD FEVER GRIPPED THE NATION in 1897, and its focal point was the Seattle waterfront, Gateway to Alaska and the Klondike. Typical scenes from those frenzied days are these of the **Willamette**, above, sailing at high noon, August 9, 1897 with 900 passengers for Dyea and the Chilkoot Trail, and the loading of the **Victoria** and **Olympia**, below, some years later.

For those who took the Nome route, the fever was frequently cooled by the Bering Sea ice, through which steamers like the little **Corwin** (opposite page) had to buck or pick their way.

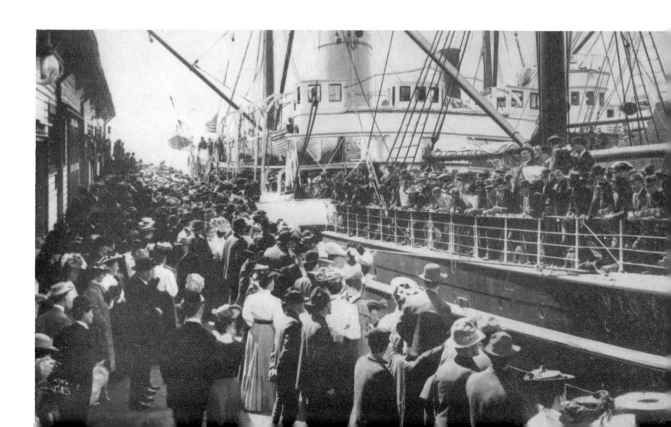

had only one driving ambition . . . to get to the Klondike as soon as possible and at any cost. Few of them knew or cared where it was; even the Seattle newspapers were vague as to its proper spelling. (Clondike and Klondyke were among the various spellings set in type in those early days.) The fact that the fabulous river was in Canada's Yukon Territory was of concern only to the underworld figures who joined the gold rush to find themselves confronted by the redcoated men of the Royal Northwest Mounted Police. Finding the mounties both incorruptible and fearless, the thieves, confidence men and crooked gamblers removed themselves to the Alaskan entry ports where they could bribe and intimidate United States marshals to their hearts' content.

For saint and sinner alike there was only one way to the gold fields of the Yukon and that was by sea . . . to Skagway or Dyea for the long overland trek by way of the Chilkoot Trail, or on to Nome and further voyaging by river steamboat up the mighty Yukon to Dawson City. The regular Alaska steamers of the Pacific Coast Company, North American Transportation and Trading Company and Charles E. Peabody's new Alaska Steamship Company, which had been cutting rates and sailing light for year, were booked solidly for months ahead.

Aspiring transportation magnates combed the boneyards and mudflats from San Pedro to Vancouver in search of anything that resembled a ship and gave promise of remaining even partially afloat for a voyage or two. Scores of new steamship companies with resounding titles sprang into existence within months of the *Portland's* dramatic arrival on Puget Sound . . .

Seattle-Yukon Transportation Company, Boston & Alaska Transportation Company, Pacific Clipper Line, The Gold Pick Line, West Coast Steam Navigation Company, Blue Star Line, Big Square Route, Seattle, St. Michael & Dawson City Transportation and Trading Company . . . and dozens more.

Seattle's mayor deserted city hall, having purchased the steamship *Humboldt*, and set himself up in business as the Humboldt Steamship Company. The Puget Sound Tug Boat Company dispatched the *Sea Lion* north towing two barges, *A-Jax* and *B-Jax*, both crammed with a pollyglot mass of freight and passengers. The *Richard Holyoke* towed the little river stern-wheeler *W. H. Merwin* all the way to Nome with a full load of passengers sealed up in the *Merwin's* boxed-in cabin. The ancient bay side-wheeler *Eliza Anderson* was hauled from the boneyard and dispatched for Nome with plenty of passengers but no compass. She blundered her way as far north as Unalaska before she fell apart on the beach.

The 45-foot steam launch *Rustler,* with a former San Francisco milk wagon driver in command, made it to Skagway with seventy passengers aboard. (She was licensed for 2ϧ

SEATTLE TIMES, which prides itself on being conservative, reported "half ton of gold" on the Portland. Post-telligencer, never agreeing with the Times on anything, boosted the count to a full ton, a figure which has taken its place in Western folklore.
... drawing by James Allan

on the placid waters of San Francisco Bay.) Captain Peabody, more restrained and conservative than his fly-by-night competitors, contented himself with advertising his pioneer Alaska Steamship Company vessel, a 136-foot Puget Sound steamboat, as the "fast and magnificent ocean steamship *Rosalie*."

Northern voyages, once marked only by the hazards of reef, storm and fog, became bold journeys during which anything might happen and frequently did. With gold dust and nuggets stacked in the purser's office, southbound Alaska steamers were tempting prey for thieves and pirates. The owners of the *Portland* took defensive action before the close of the 1897 Nome season, proudly announcing that they had purchased a Maxim rapid-fire gun to be mounted on their steamer's bow. The Seattle *Times*, which had earlier been "against" the Alaska gold rush, had bowed to the inevitable and was reporting the fantastic doings with great gusto. It had this to say about the *Portland's* new-fangled armament:

"The Maxim gun is the very latest device for killing people in rapid succession. It is oper-

ated by one man and is capable of discharging 600 cartridges per minute. The gun can be set at any angle required and can be made to oscillate continually and rapidly over an arc, sweeping any common enemy from in front of it, much after the fashion of a mowing machine eating a pathway through a field of ripened clover.

When the *Portland* arrives here, the weapon of destruction will be mounted on a tripod on her bow, prepared to give pirates, whether from the Chinese empire or from the Malay peninsula, a torrid reception. A party attempting to board the treasure ship with the gun in working order wolud be impeded by a stream of blood which would make a footing on the deck difficult, if the rain of bullets did not stop them."

In that pre-atomic age of innocence, the blood-thirsty reports of the terrible Maxim gun were widely printed, adding new fuel to the flames of gold fever, although there is no record of piratical boarding parties attacking the Alaska ships. There were numerous gold robberies, but most of them were inside jobs. A messboy on the *City of Seattle* managed to lug eight gold bars ashore before he was nabbed and a gang looted fifty thousand dollars worth of bullion from the *Humboldt*. Actually the losses through robbery and theft were minor, considering the motely crowds who flocked to board the Nome and Skagway liners.

There were poets, like Robert Service and that bard of the Sierras and veteran of California's 1849 gold rush, Joaquin Miller, who departed for Dyea on the *Mexico* loudly proclaiming his delight at leaving "insane Seattle." There were confidence men and bunco-steerers like the legendary Soapy Smith and such unsavory henchmen as Judge Van Horn, Doc Baggs and the Reverend Bowers. There were gambling men like Bob Howard, "The Dirty Little Coward who Killed Mr. Howard and Laid Jessie James in His Grave," Tex Rickard and Wilson Mizner. There were women, too, running the gamut from "Susie Bluenose," a far-northern Carrie Nation who carried on a one-woman crusade against hard liquor, to such denizens of the Northern-lights districts of Lousetown in Klondike City and Paradise Alley in Dawson as Nellie the Pig, Diamond-Tooth Gertie and the Oregon Mare.

Some of the crew members of the northern coastwise liners jumped ship at the Alaska ports and joined the Klondike stampede, just as sailors had done in 1849 along the California coast. Some of them died of scurvy or exposure or typhoid. Some were simply rolled by Soapy Smith's boys in Skagway and returned thankfully to the foc'sle of the first south-bound steamer they could sign aboard. A few, like Kate Mulrooney, erstwhile stewardess on the *City of Topeka*, made their fortunes. Kate made a pierhead jump from the *Topeka* at Skagway early in the rush and established a road house at the forks of Eldorado and Bonanza Creeks. Establishing a policy of good food, clean bunks and reasonable prices, she soon owned a chain of profitable roadhouses, shares in some of the area's richest mining claims and a French count named Carboneau.

Just as Irish Kate entered the gold rush a stewardess on coastwise liners and emerged from it a countess with a million dollars in the bank, the territory of Alaska, purchased from Russia for a half-cent an acre less than a generation earlier, became an important adjunct to the continental United States. As the gold fever died out, most of the spur-of-the-moment steamship companies faded from the scene, but the Alaska coastal route had become an estab-

The motto of shipping men during gold rush days was "If it floats it will pay dividends." Western newspapers were full of advertisements like these, extolling the virtues of a motely fleet of gold rush ships . . .
. . . there were flat-bottomed stern-wheel steamboats like

lished one. Gone were the days of isolated sailings by a few old steamers like the *Ancon*, the *Idaho* and the *Mexico*.

. . . there were flat-bottomed stern-wheel steamboats like the **Victorian**, above

. . . and tired old side-wheelers with decades of bay and river steaming behind them, like the **Geo. E. Starr,** below.

There were old-timers like the **Bellingham,** first ship of the Alaska Line, above,
. . . little bay steamboats like the **Utopia,** which once hauled hay, grain and passengers on Puget Sound for the
La Conner Trading & Transportation Company . . .

. . . the **Rosalie,** built for Alameda ferry service,

. . . and the **Discovery,** built at Port Townsend in 1889 as a tugboat and destined for violent death in a Gulf of Alaska hurricane of 1903, taking all hands down with her.

There were tiny gas schooners like the **Silver Wave**, left, and **Sea Wolf**, right.

... there were even big deep-sea liners like the **Victoria** and **Olympia**, below.

Above, **Victoria.**

At the Seattle docks in springtime the decks of the Alaska steamers were alive with activity and bets were placed on favorite ships expected to be first through the ice to Nome. Steam sobbed from the brass throats of the whistles . . .

Right, **Al Ki.**

. . . and the gold rush ships sailed north.

Left, Captain Hunter on bridge of **Farallon**. Below, Mates **Herbingot** and Busse of the first **Alaska**.

Columbia Glacier

(**Dora** at Columbia Glacier)

. . . Past glittering mountains of age-old glacial ice,

. . . and through the cold darkness of Arctic storms.

Some of the treasure seekers pressed north to Nome and the Arctic Circle, the ships of the gold rush pitting the power of steam and iron against the deadly grip of the great ice pack.

Ohio - 1903

(Above and opposite, **Ohio**).
(**Oregon**)

. . . Some preferred the grim overland trail to the Klondike. They left the ships at Skagway or Dyea, where there were docks to receive men and supplies.

(Rosalie at Skagway)

(**Nome City** in Bering Sea)

. . . Those who went to Nome might walk ashore on ice, or ferry across treacherous Nome Roadstead by lighter to the red sands of the beach.

(St. Paul in Nome Roadstead)

(Princess May wreck)

(Townsend wreck)

. . . And some of the gold rush ships made no port at all.

GOLD RUSH SHIPS

Left, top to bottom: **Portland** started it all when she brought a ton of gold to Schwabacker's Wharf, Seattle. **Humboldt** was on the ways as a lumber schooner when gold rush struck, was rushed to completion as a passenger ship. **Nome City,** 900-ton wooden passenger steamer was built at Fairhaven, California in 1900 especially for the Nome trade. After four years operation by the Pacific Clipper Line in this service, she was cut down to steam schooner specifications; hauled lumber for Charles Nelson & Company until about 1930. **Ohio,** built by Cramp of Philadelphia in 1873 as trans-Atlantic passenger steamer, and was brought around the Horn for Nome service of Empire Transportation Company in spring of 1898. Struck reef in Millbank Sound and sank with loss of three lives in 1909 while in Alaska Line service.

Right, top to bottom: **Garonne,** one of first refrigerated ships in British Merchant Navy, engaged in gold rush traffic, then departed in 1905 to run Japanese blockade carrying Russian refugees from Port Arthur. **Morgan City,** purchased in New York by Joe Ladue, founder of Dawson City for Seattle-St. Michael run, was taken over by government in June, 1898 as Spanish War transport. **Maneuence** was another of the ocean steamers chartered for brief Alaska service during gold rush height.

GOLD RUSH SHIPS

Left, top to bottom: **Cottage City,** wooden passenger steamer of 1885 gross tons, built at Bath, Maine in 1890, operating until 1899 on New York-Portland, Maine route. Wrecked at Cape Mudge, January, 1911. **City of Topeka,** iron passenger steamer, 1057 gross tons, built at Chester, Pa. in 1884. **Al Ki,** wooden steamer, 1259 gross tons, built at Bath, Maine in 1884. Right, top to bottom: **Hyades** was 3753 gross ton steel freighter built at Sparrow's Point, Md. in 1900; served Alaska coastal routes briefly during height of gold rush. **Yucaton,** sister-ship of **Orizaba** (2) was brought west for Alaska trade in 1906, three years later was converted to luxury yacht for cruise of J. P. Morgan, Simon Guggenheim and other financiers to Alaska. Back in Alaska Line passenger service, she struck an ice berg in Icy Straits the following year, was eventually raised and converted to freighter running from San Francisco to Mexican ports. **Dirigo,** pioneer passenger carrier of Alaska Line, was cut down to steam schooner rig following 1899 stranding south of Juneau, was primarily a freight carrier for most of her career. In 1914 given added passenger accommodations for Cook Inlet run, but foundered in open sea off Cape Spencer soon afterward. **Victorian,** built as Sound luxury steamer by Oregon Railway & Navigation Company, made Alaska voyages during gold rush; was plagued by high operating costs and frequent breakdowns.

GOLD RUSH SHIPS

Left, top to bottom: **Delhi** was built for Pacific Coast Steamship Company at Hall Brothers' Puget Sound yard especially for Alaskan trade. A 237-foot steam schooner, she carried 30 first class, 18 second class passengers; wrecked in Sumner Strait, Alaska, 1915. **James Dollar,** built in 1900 as **John S. Kimball,** served Alaska Line as **Santa Clara** from 1905 to 1909. Was wrecked off Oregon Coast in 1915. **Jeanie,** built at Bath, Maine in 1883, ran on nearly all routes from San Francisco to Nome from 1888 until her loss in Queen Charlotte Sound in 1913. While in Pacific Steam Whaling Company service her hull was sheathed with Australian iron bark for Arctic service. **Corwin,** former revenue cutter, was frequently "first boat to Nome" in gold rush days.

Right, top to bottom: **Olympia,** British-built in 1883 as **Dunbar Casles,** served Alaska routes from 1904 until wrecked in 1910. **Oregon** was in Alaska trade from 1900 until wrecked in 1906 under White Star and Northwestern Steamship Co. ownership. **Saratoga** was an iron steamer built on the East Coast in 1878. Wrecked in Alaskan waters in 1908.

GOLD RUSH SHIPS

Left, top to bottom: **Roanoke** and **Oregon** at Seattle with last of cargo coming aboard and steam up for first-of-season race to Nome. **Elihu Thompson** was transpacific steamer diverted to gold rush service for "Big Square Route" to Nome; later became refrigerated freighter nicknamed "Alaska's meat wagon." **Islander**, British-built flagship of Canadian Pacific Navigation Co., struck berg and sank with heavy loss of life shortly after coming under Canadian Pacific Railway ownership in 1901. Legends of fabulous gold treasure aboard persisted for more than a generation.

Right, top to bottom: **Centennial**, ancient iron liner built in England, 1859, as P & O **Delta**. Sold, 1874, to Japan as **Takasago Maru**, and to American owners in gold rush days. After career as Russo-Japanese war blockade runner, went missing in the Pacific, was sighted years later imprisoned in ice in the Okhotsk Sea. **City of Seattle** at Skagway during career as gold rush ship. **Dirigo** in Quatermaster Harbor drydock, 1900. Engineers Roy Bruce and Lee Nellis is foreground.

UNINSPIRING WELCOME FOR KLONDIKE STAMPEDERS was provided by Skagway's muddy main street, above, or that beehive of confusion, the Dyea freight yard, below, where cargo from incoming ships was dumped for passengers to reclaim as best they could.

Opposite page: Veteran Alaska packet **Dora,** above, rigged in early days as steam brigantine, made voyages to isolated western Alaska and Aleutian Island ports like the landing shown in lower photo, taken from her deck. Stranded and lost in Alert Bay in December, 1920.

HARDSHIP AND PERIL MARKED EARLY GOLD RUSH DAYS as Cheechaco (tenderfoot) gold-seekers tackled the man-killing overland route from Skagway and Dyea to the gold fields of the interior. The upper photo shows the long line of human pack-horses ascending the Chilkoot Trail, the lower view is of the summit of Chilkoot Pass.

IRON HORSE IN THE FAR NORTH, ended worst of gold rush hardships. The White Pass and Yukon Railway was completed in 1899 and wood-burning diamond-stackers like the one that hauled the first passenger train over White Pass summit (above) made things much easier for those who embarked on overcrowded steamers like the **Al Ki,** below

SEATTLE POST-INTELLIGENCE

SEATTLE, WASHINGTON, WEDNESDAY, AUGUST 4, 1897.   TWELVE-PAGE ED

AN EVERY-DAY SCENE IN SEATTLE.

The Steamship Al-Ki Sailed Yesterday for Dyea. During the Day the Wharf Was Crowded With People, Drays Loaded With Merchandise, and Cattle and Horses. When the Al-Ki Pulled Away From the Dock Every Available Space Was Occupied.

PASSAGE TO GOLD FIELDS FROM NOME was by river steamboat up the Yukon River. Above, passengers from an early-season Nome liner are pictured trekking ashore over the ice floe to which the ship is moored. When the roadstead was clear of ice, men, supplies and animals were ferried ashore by lighter, below.

SUDDEN ARCTIC STORMS whip up angry rollers in the shallow Bering Sea, above, and exposed Nome Roadstead, below, claimed its share of ships and men. The dramatic photograph below shows the Nome lifesaving crew fighting seas to rescue the crew of the little sloop Greyhound, while larger ships, partly obscured by storm mists, work seaward to ride out the storm.

Captain Joe Dodge of the **Alaska**.

STRANGE TALE OF THE S.S. HUMBOLDT

The little wooden steamer *Humboldt* (213 feet long, 688 net tons) was designed as a coastwise lumber carrier, but the great Alaska gold rush prompted her conversion to a passenger liner upon her launching at Eureka in 1897. She made her first Alaska voyage that summer; by 1915 had completed her five hundredth. In this perilous service the *Humboldt* suffered only one serious mishap, striking a reef near Victoria during a dense fog on the morning of September 29, 1908. For some time it was feared she would break up, but eventually she was gotten off and returned to service.

Captain Elijah G. Baughman was the *Humboldt's* pilot on her first voyage to Skagway. In 1900 he was appointed master and he remained with the *Humboldt* throughout his entire career as a shipmaster.

By 1933 the old *Humboldt* had been relegated to a dreary mooring in the San Diego boneyard; Captain Baughman had retired and was living ashore in San Francisco. Lonely and deserted, the old Alaska treasure ship lay quietly at anchor for two years . . . until the night of August 8, 1935.

That was the night Captain Baughman died . . . slipped his cable, as oldtime sailors used to say. And it was the night the *Humboldt* slipped her cable, too, and sailed again for the last time. Toward midnight, a Coast Guard cutter hailed an unlighted ship moving silently through the harbor. It was the *Humboldt*, out of the boneyard at last and heading, with eerie precision, toward the open sea.

The Coast Guard boarded her and found her warped decks and dusty cabins deserted. They marked it down as a freak of wind and current and towed the *Humboldt* back to the ship's graveyard.

No living hand, surely, guided the *Humboldt* that night, but the relationship between a man and a ship who have lived their lives together can become a strangely mystic one. And there are more things on heaven and earth . . . and on the sea . . . than our philosophy has dreamed of.

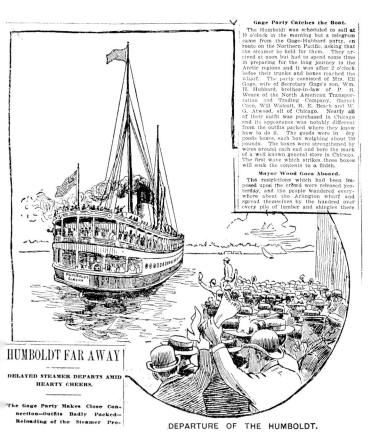

Gage Party Catches the Boat.

The Humboldt was scheduled to sail at 10 o'clock in the morning but a telegram came from the Gage-Hubbard party, en route on the Northern Pacific, asking that the steamer be held for them. They arrived at noon but had to spend some time in preparing for the long journey to the Arctic regions and it was after 2 o'clock befoe their trunks and boxes reached the wharf. The party consisted of Mrs. Elli Gage, wife of Secretary Gage's son, Wm. H. Hubbard, brother-in-law of P. B. Weare of the North American Transportation and Trading Company, Garnet Coen, Will Walcott, R. E. Beach and W. G. Atwood, all of Chicago. Nearly all of their outfit was purchased in Chicago and its appearance was notably different from the outfits packed where they know how to do it. The goods were in dry goods boxes, each box weighing about 750 pounds. The boxes were strengthened by wires around each end and bore the mark of a well known general store in Chicago. The first wave which strikes those boxes will soak the contents to a finish.

Mayor Wood Goes Aboard.

The restrictions which had been imposed upon the crowd were released yesterday, and the people wandered everywhere about the Arlington wharf and spread themselves by the hundred over every pile of lumber and shingles there

HUMBOLDT FAR AWAY

DELAYED STEAMER DEPARTS AMID HEARTY CHEERS.

The Gage Party Makes Close Connection—Outfits Badly Packed—Reloading of the Steamer Pro-

DEPARTURE OF THE HUMBOLDT.

ALASKA STEAM

Of the more than a hundred steamship companies which have operated between American West Coast ports and Alaska since gold rush days, only one has survived; the Alaska Steamship Company of Seattle.

More than competition by other transportation media accounts for the high mortality rate among far north shipping companies . . . and among the vessels they operated. In 1947 a member of the United States Maritime Commission, testifying before a congressional committee, had this to say about the business of running steamships to Alaska:

"I personally asked at least 25 principal steamship companies if they could possibly be induced, under any circumstances, to enter the Alaska trade. Replies ranged from a horse laugh to 'Nuts.' That generally is considered as one of the least desirable trades anyone would want to be in."

Alaska's tremendous size is a major problem in itself. Dwarfing Texas, this forty-ninth state sprawls across nearly six hundred thousand square miles of the earth's surface, yet its total population, excluding military personnel, is less than that of Fall River or Phoenix. To serve this tiny population of a mighty land, steamships must call at 92 ports, the closest, Ketchikan, 750 miles north of Seattle; the furthest, Kotzebue, above the Arctic Circle 2850 miles from Puget Sound.

And these ports are separated from the rest of the United States and from ane another by a watery labyrinth of islands, straits, glaciers, rock-studded passes, sheltered waterways and reaches of open sea. This sea road to the north is beset by fog, blizzards, floating icebergs, hidden pinnacle rocks, sudden raging Arctic storms and tidal bores which sweep through narrow passes with the velocity and power of tidal waves.

The steamship company which has survived these hazards for more than half a century was born of modest circumstances in 1895 . . . two years before the great Alaska gold rush.[1] Charles E. Peabody and associates inaugurated the Alaska Steamship Company with a single vessel, the little *Willapa,* formerly the Oregon & Coast Steamship Company's Columbia-Grays Harbor packet *General Miles.*

The infant shipping company bravely declared war on the mighty Pacific Coast Steamship Company, which had been maintaining a comfortable monopoly rate of fifty dollars a passenger and eleven dollars per ton of freight on the Seattle-Juneau run. The *Willapa* reduced passenger fares to twelve dollars and freight rates to three dollars a ton. Pacific Coast Steam reacted in the manner of an elephant stung on the rump by a gadfly. Fares on their *City of Topeka* and *Queen* were reduced to meet the *Willapa's* tariff, while rates for their *Mexico* were reduced even lower. The big *Mexico* did nothing but hound the poor little *Willapa,* following her wherever she went and under-bidding her passenger fares and freight rates at every port of call.

[1] Some old-time Alaska sourdoughs credited the Alaska Steamship Company with having started the gold rush. The Seattle **Post-Intelligencer,** on August 7, 1897 published this contemporary opinion: "The sudden rush to the Klondike of gold seekers has made W. R. Elliott of this city somewhat reminiscent, and he attributes the finds on the Klondike and the prosperity which has followed in its wake to a very humble source. 'I believe,' said he today, 'that the gold of the Klondike would never have been discovered had not the steamer **Willapa** entered the Alaska trade as an opposition steamer to those of the Pacific Coast Steamship Company. The reduced fares in consequence of competition resulted in many people flocking to the north, and most of those who went to the Yukon were enabled to do so simply on account of the comparatively low cost. If it had not been for the **Willapa** there would have been no very great traffic to Alaska, and the people today would not have known of the great natural wealth of the territory. If it had not been for the **Willapa** I would not have gone north, because I could not have afforded the trip, and the majority of the people in Alaska today, if they tell the truth, will say the same thing'."

AN "AISLE OF ISLES," the Inside Passage to Alaska, is viewed by passengers from the boat deck of the Alaska Steamship Company's **Aleutian**. . . . H. J. Keeler photo

This state of affairs continued until March of 1896, when the *Willapa* went ashore in the north and was given up as lost[2]. Even this disaster failed to put the new firm out of business for long. Before the Klondike rush was under way, the Alaska Steamship Company had purchased the little steamer *Rosalie*, built in 1893 for the San Francisco-Vallejo ferry run. As business increased, the *Alliance* was added to the fleet as a chartered vessel. The *Dirigo* and *Farallon* were purchased in 1899, these four ships constituting the line's modest fleet throughout the gold rush era. The *Dirigo*, at the time of her purchase, was a typical small passenger steamer, but soon thereafter she was

2 In a later salvage attempt the **Willapa** was refloated and sold to the Canadian Pacific Navigation Company, in whose service she remained until 1902, when she was sold American again as a unit of the Thompson Steamboat Company on Puget Sound, where she received her third and final name, **Bellingham**. In less than a year she reverted to Peabody ownership again, when his Alaska Steamship Company bought out Captain John Rex Thompson's Sound fleet. Under this name she remained in service until after World War II; was burned at the Seattle Seafair of 1950.

wrecked south of Juneau while under command of Captain George Roberts, one of the company's founders, who had an unfortunate proclivity for putting to sea just ahead of violent storms. When she was salvaged the *Dirigo* was cut down to the steam schooner specifications of the *Farallon* and the two were the Alaska Line's first freight-hauling workhorses, although they maintained limited passenger accommodations until the end of their long service with the company.

The line's first bid for a share in the first class passenger trade came with the purchase of the *Dolphin* in 1900 and the charter of the *Humboldt* to operate with her. In 1904 the *Jefferson*, the only brand-new passenger steamer ever to enter the Alaska Line's service, was launched at Tacoma for the Southern Alaska express service. She was the first vessel of the fleet to exceed a thousand tons.

In 1903 Pabody had combined his recently purchased Thompson Steamboat Company fleet

AGE-OLD ICE WALL of Taku Glacier glides past slowly steaming Alaska cruise liner Denali.

... H. J. Keeler photo

of Puget Sound vessels, along with the pioneer *Rosalie,* with Joshua Green's La Conner Trading & Transportation Company fleet to form the Puget Sound Navigation Company, so in 1908 the original Alaska Steamship Company was still operating a four-ship fleet, the *Dirigo, Farallon, Dolphin* and *Jefferson.* Before the year was over fifteen steamers were flying the Alaska Steam houseflag as the result of a merger between Peabody's company and the Northwestern Steamship Company.

Organized in 1904 by John Rosene and his associates of the Northwestern Commercial Company, the Northwestern Steamship Company was, in 1908, owned by the Guggenheim-Morgan copper interests. Its fleet list at the time of the merger included the *Dora, Edith, Northwestern, Oakland, Olympia, Pennsylvania, Saratoga, Santa Ana, Santa Clara, Seward, Yucatan* and *Victoria.* Although then a minority stockholder, Peabody remained as president

of the combined companies until 1910, when he transferred his active participation to the Puget Sound Navigation Company, where he remained in partnership with Joshua Green for a quarter of a century.

In 1915 the company came under the ownership of Kennecott Copper Company, which operated the line until World War II.

In August, 1944, ownership of the Alaska Steamship Company was transferred to the Skinner & Eddy Corporation of Seattle, the line's present owners. Traditional passenger steamship service continued until September, 1954. That month the *Denali,* last passenger ship to be added to the fleet, made the last passenger-carrying voyage from Seattle to Alaska. The tremendous post-war rise in operating costs, coupled with air, highway and military transport competition had made continuation of the service financially impossible. Throughout their history, the Alaska Liners had never enjoyed a government subsidy.

SHIPS OF ALASKA STEAM

Left, top to bottom: Willapa, built 1882 as General Miles, was first unit of fleet in 1895. Wrecked 1897, later operated by Canadian Pacific and Puget Sound Navigation Co. as Bellingham. Rosalie, built 1893, in Alaska Line service 1897-1900. Burned at Seattle, 1918. Dirigo, built 1898, in fleet from 1899-1914 when sunk in Alaskan waters while being towed. Farallon, built 1888 and in service 1899-1910, when wrecked in Alaska (page 181).

Right, top to bottom: Dolphin, built 1892 as Al Foster. In service 1900-1917, when sold for Chilean coast service, later converted to gunboat. Jefferson, built for company at Tacoma, 1904. In service until scrapped in 1925. Olympia, British-built, 1883, as Dunbar Castle. Iron hull, compound engine. In service 1904-1910, when wrecked in Alaska.

ALASKA STEAM

Left, top to bottom: **Victoria,** British-built, 1870, as Cunard Line **Parthia** (1). In service 1904-1954, when converted to Canadian barge. Towed to Japan for scrapping, 1956. (see page 163.) **Dora,** built 1880, wood hull, compound engine. In service 1905-1918. Wrecked in British Columbia, 1920. **Oakland,** 1905-1911, was small wooden freighter, gasoline engine. Wrecked in Alaska, 1912.

Right, top to bottom: **Santa Ana,** built 1900, in service 1905-1923. Sold to East Coast and burned in 1939. **Santa Clara,** built 1900 as **J. S. Kimball,** later **James Dollar,** in service 1905-1909. Wrecked off Oregon coast, 1915. **Edith,** iron hull, compound engine, built 1882 as **Glenochil.** In service 1905-1915, when lost off Alaska. **Pennsylvania,** iron passenger liner, built 1873 and in company service 1905-1909. Burned in 1918.

SHIPS OF ALASKA STEAM

Left, top to bottom: **Saratoga**, iron, compound engine, built 1878 and in service 1906-1908, when wrecked in Alaska. **Northwestern**, built 1889 as **Orizaba** (2). In service 1906-1938. Used as barracks ship at Dutch Harbor in World War 2, bombed by Japanese aircraft. **Yucatan**, built 1890 and in Alaska service 1906 to 1910, when wrecked, sold and rebuilt as freighter. Last name of record **Shinkai Maru**, under Japanese ownership. **Seward**, in service from construction in 1907 to 1916. Sold as Army transport and torpedoed off France in 1917.

Right, top to bottom: **Ohio**, iron passenger liner built in 1873. In service 1908-1909. Wrecked in British Columbia waters, 1909. **Latouche**, built 1910 and in service until sold to Philippine owners, 1939. **Alameda**, iron transpacific liner built 1883 and purchased 1910. Burned at Seattle, 1931.

ALASKA STEAM

Left, top to bottom: **Mariposa,** built 1883 and similar to **Alameda.** In service 1911-1917, when wrecked in Alaskan waters. **Cordova,** purchased before completion as lumber schooner, 1912 and completed as passenger-freighter. Sold to Chinese owners, 1947, renamed **Lee Kung. Alaska** (old), built 1889 as **Kansas City.** In service 1915-1921, when wrecked off California coast while chartered to San Francisco-Portland S.S. Co.

Right, top to bottom: **Redondo,** built 1902, in service 1915-1935 when converted to barge. Sank in California, 1948. **Valdez,** built 1908 as **Bennington.** In service as freighter, 1915-1923. **Juneau,** built 1908 as **Burlington.** Same service and dates as Valdez, above. **Ketchikan,** built 1899 as Pacific Coast Steam's **Eureka** (2), in service 1916-1937. Renamed **Nizina,** 1926. Scrapped in Japan.

SHIPS OF ALASKA STEAM

Left, top to bottom: **Alaska** (new), built for company 1923; twin screw, turbo-electric. Sold 1955 and scrapped after short, unprofitable career as cruise liner **Mazatlan**. Yukon, built 1899 as **Mexico** (later **Colon**). In service 1924 until 1946, when wrecked in Alaska. **Denali** (2) twin-crew turbine steamer, built 1927 as **Caracas**. Purchased in 1938 and given name of company freighter wrecked in 1920. Sold on suspension of passenger service in 1954, renamed **Cuba**. Scrapped. **Aleutian** (2), built 1906 as **Mexico**, purchased 1930 to replace first **Aleutian**, wrecked the previous year. Sold in 1954 and after short career as cruise ship **Tradewinds** sold to Japan for scrap.

Right, top to bottom: **Dellwood**, built 1919 as Army cable ship. In service 1932-1943, when wrecked in Alaska. **Kenai**, built 1904 as Army mineplanter **Mifflin** was smallest of Alaska Line fleet, serving as feeder boat to isolated ports, 1934-1942. Converted to tug and presently a hulk at Foss Seattle moorings. **Starr,** built 1912 as halibut fishing steamer, served feeder ports 1935-1940, when sold for scrap.

ALASKA STEAM

Left, top to bottom: Bering, World War 1 wooden ship built 1918 as Annette Rolph, later Arthur J. Baldwin. In service 1938 until 1943 when she struck Alaska reef, was declared total loss. Towed to Seattle and still on the beach at entrance to government ship canal. Baranof, built 1919 as Santa Elisa, in service 1936 until layed up and scrapped 1956. Mount McKinley, built 1918 as Santa Luisa. In service 1936 until wrecked in Alaska, 1942.

Right, top to bottom: Columbia, built 1907 as President, later Dorothy Alexander. In service 1937-1946, when sold and renamed Portugal. Scrapped, Italy, 1952. Caracas as she appeared on arrival at Seattle for conversion to Alaska cruise liner Denali. Two lower photos illustrate type of vessel operated by Alaska Steam in freight service since abandonment of passenger operations. Chena is World War 2 liberty ship (ex-Chief Washakie) especially rebuilt for efficient unitized freight shipment. Susitna is wartime coastal motorship class (ex-Terminal Knot).

OLD-TIMERS LIKE THE JEFFERSON, above, had ornate interior decorations, as typified by carved stairway, left, and, on opposite page, dining salon and hallway views. **Alaska** (2) of 1923, had more functional interior design. (Right column, opposite page)

Capt. Connell was veteran Alaska Line skipper.

COMFORT AFLOAT

IN PASSENGER-CARRYING DAYS, Alaska liners docked in heart of downtown Seattle in the shadow of the 42-story Smith Tower, tallest West Coast office building, above, dodged cross-Sound ferries on arrival and departure, below.

ALASKA CRUISE PASSENGERS ENJOYED DANCING on ships like the **Aleutian**, above, or the former California liner **President**, shown below headed north from Seattle as the Alaska Line's **Columbia**.

The scenery was fun, too. Airline passengers get there quicker, but miss views like these of Inside Passage grandeur, above, and thrill of negotiating Wrangell Narrows, below.

S.S. NORTHWESTERN at Cordova, Alaska pier in postgold rush year of 1912.

... Photo Courtesy Jack Dillon

SCENIC BEAUTIES HID NAVIGATIONAL PERILS, however, and sometimes liners like the Alaska, below, bumped their noses and had to undergo drydock surgery before resuming their duties.

ICE IS ALL RIGHT IN ITS PLACE, in the form of glaciers which provided spectacular viewing for passengers on the Dolphin, above, but it was sometimes a problem to the crews of the northern liners when it took over the ship, as shown below.

Chipping ice was no fun for the Aleutian's deck hand, above, but the northern voyages had their compensations. Where else could you pick up a Kodiak bear cub for ship's mascot? (below)

"SOAPY SMITH'S STREETCAR," above, met incoming steamers at Skagway, bearing fearsome likeness of the gold rush bad man on the rear platform.

SAILING DAY MEANT EXCITEMENT in the Good Old Days of not so long ago. The bustle of embarkation and the Blue Peter flying at the foremast, opposite. Gay shipboard parties and the thrill of ocean sunsets, left. Right, above and lower, the Denali ends the era as she makes last departure from Pier 42, Seattle at 3 p.m., September 24, 1954.

SADLY MISSING FROM ALASK PORTS like Metlakatla, above, and Yakutat, below, are the passenger liners of Alaska Steam, which sailed that way for almost sixty years. The **Alaska** is pictured above, **Columbia** below.

. . . H. J. Keeler photos

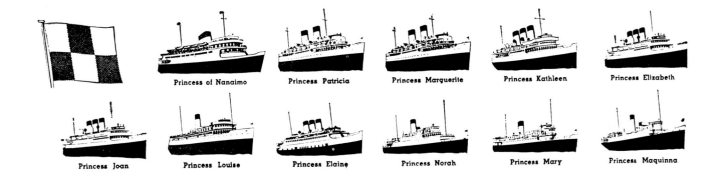

Princess of Nanaimo   Princess Patricia   Princess Marguerite   Princess Kathleen   Princess Elizabeth

Princess Joan   Princess Louise   Princess Elaine   Princess Norah   Princess Mary   Princess Maquinna

CANADIAN PACIFIC

Although the Canadian Pacific Railway was not the first company to operate regularly scheduled passenger steamers on British Columbia coastal routes—(Union Steamships has gained its solid place in history on that score)—the CPR Pacific coastal fleet has pioneer antecedents, for it can trace its pedigree clear back to the legendary side-wheeler *Beaver,* first steamship to ply the waters of the American Pacific Coast.

The Hudson's Bay Company, which brought the *Beaver* out from England in 1836, operated a number of steamships from Alaska to San Francisco over the following years, but on company business and not as scheduled, passenger-carrying liners. In 1883, however, a syndicate headed by Commodore John Irving merged with the Hudson's Bay Company's marine division to form the Canadian Pacific Navigation Company. Immediate steps were taken to provide freight and passenger service to British Columbia coastal settlements which were expected to boom with the coming of the Canadian Pacific Railway's trans-continental line from the East.

Surveys for the Pacific Coast section of CPR had begun back in 1871; the first passenger train rolled into Port Moody, first Pacific Coast terminus for the line, in the late fall of 1885. Less than two years later the line was extended the additional 13 miles to Vancouver, the first transcontinental passenger train arriving at the Granville Street station on May 23, 1887. The company discovered early in the game that the steamboat was an essential ally to the iron horse in conquering the rugged terraine of western Canada. The first CPR boat to operate in the West was the little stern-wheeler *Skuzzy,* whose arrival on the scene was described as follows by George B. Abdill in his book *This Was Railroading* (Superior Publishing Company, Seattle, 1958):

"While Major Rogers was probing the desolate Selkirk Range, Andrew Onderdonk's army hacked their way up the Fraser. About seven thousand men signed his payroll and toiled along the line. In the 60-odd mile section between Yale and Lytton they bored 15 tunnels, one of them 1,600 feet long. So rugged was the nature of the canyon that men were lowered by ropes to drill holes for blasting in the sheer rock walls. All supplies had to be packed in on horses and mules, creating such a problem that a plant was set up between Yale and Emory to manufacture dynamite on the spot. Onderdonk determined to build a steamboat to run up through the Grand Canyon of the Fraser to operate on the navigable waters above.

"The craft was constructed by a master shipwright, William Dalton, and was named the *Skuzzy.* She was a stern-wheeler 120 feet long, with a 20-compartment watertight hull. In addition to her powerful engines that cranked her paddles, she had a steam winch or capstan placed on her bows, driven by two engines, to enable her to 'line over' the rapids. Onderdonk secured the services of Captains S. R. and David Smith, notable white-water pilots from the Columbia River in Oregon. Capt. S. R. Smith, with Engineer J. W. Burse and a crew of 17 men, successfully hauled the *Skuzzy* through Black Canyon and Hell Gate, arriving in a battered but serviceable condition at Boston Bar. The trip had taken two weeks and the hardest battle with the roaring currents of the Fraser had occurred at China Riffle; here, in addition to the powerful thrust of her big stern-wheel, the steam winch and a crew of 15 men at a capstan, it was necessary to enlist 150 Chinamen, tugging on a third hawser, to line up over the ripads."

Nothing daunted by this rugged introduction to Western steamboating, Canadian Pacific Railway, in 1890, bought the Columbia and Koote-

PRINCESS MARGUERITE

nay River Navigation Company, thus entering its long and picturesque era of paddleboat operation on the upper Columbia. The following year, 1891, the railway placed its beautiful, yachtlike *Empress of India, Empress of China* and *Empress of Japan* in trans-Pacific service between the Orient and CPR's West Coast terminus at Vancouver.

It was not until 1901, however, that the big railway company entered the British Columbia coastal service. That year it bought all the stock of the Canadian Pacific Navigation Company, along with its fleet, which included the steamers *Islander, Charmer, Tees, Danube, Amur, Otter, Queen City, Willapa, Maude,* the side-wheelers *Yosemite* and *Princess Louise,* and the stern-wheelers *R. P. Rithet, Beaver (2)* and *Transfer.*

This hodgepodge fleet of small and, in some cases, antiquated craft, didn't meet the specifications of the railway company, which was fast becoming a mighty power in the Northwest. Only two of the ships, the *Islander* and *Charmer,* exceeded a thousand gross tons, and the *Islander,* flagship and pride of the fleet, met her tragic end even before she could hoist CPR's red and white checkered houseflag.

To fill immediate needs, the company purchased the old China coaster *Ningchow,* a twin-screw liner of 1394 gross tons, which had operated in a variety of services under several names since her launching at Newcastle on Tyne in 1888. Apparently the railway company took a hint from the oldest unit of the Canadian Pacific Navigation Company fleet, the *Princess Louise,* of 1869, for the *Ningchow* was renamed *Princess May,* and all but three of the thirty-odd CPR coastal liners which followed were *Princesses.*[1]

The *Princess May,* in later years, distinguished herself by escaping almost unscathed from what was probably the most spectacular shipwreck in West Coast history (page 169). During most of her CPR career the *Princess May* operated between Vancouver and southeastern Alaska ports.

On January 21, 1904, the Seattle *Times* reported the following transportation development:

"Canadian Pacific Railroad Company's fine new steamship *Princess Beatrice* left yesterday at 9:30 a.m. from Pier No. 2 on her first trip to Victoria. The vessel arrived here Monday

---

1 The exceptions were the **Joan, Nootka** and **City of Nanaimo,** all purchased "second-hand" and retained in service for limited periods.

night and was prepared for her maiden trip on the new run. She is scheduled to leave Seattle at 9:30 o'clock each morning, and, returning, leave Victoria at 11 o'clock each night, except Sunday. This makes it very convenient for all passengers coming from Tacoma and other valley points, so that they can leave home at a reasonable hour and take the boat from Victoria. She took a good list of passengers yesterday and the officials of the Canadian Pacific are much pleased at the start."

Thus began year-around steamer service between Seattle and British Columbia, inaugurated by the 1290-ton wooden *Princess Beatrice*, built for CPR by British Columbia Marine Railway at Victoria in 1903. It was a service which was to continue virtually uninterrupted for well over half a century. The Seattle *Times* covered the story when, on February 25, 1959, the final winter sailing was made by the *Princess Elizabeth*:

"The steamship *Princess Elizabeth*. long a familiar sight on the Seattle waterfront, pulled away from the Canadian Pacific dock at the foot of Lenora Street yesterday on her final trip to Canada. CPR is discontinuing winter service between Seattle, Victoria and Vancouver, B.C., and the *Princess Joan* and *Princess Elizabeth* are being retired permanently[2]. The steamship company will resume summer service in mid-May, with the *Princess Marguerite* and *Princess Patricia* on the Seattle-Victoria-Vancouver run. Other vessels in Elliott Bay gave the departing passenger ship the traditional three-whistle salute."

The original Seattle-Victoria run of the *Princess Beatrice* was expanded to become the Seattle-Victoria-Vancouver triangle service with the arrival, in 1904, of the fleet and graceful *Princess Victoria*, launched at the Swan & Hunter yard at Newcastle in late December of 1902. Destined to become one of the West Coast's legendary liners, the *Princess Vic*, as she came to be affectionately known, was a twin-screw steel steamship, equipped with a 6000-horsepower reciprocating engine that could push her along easily at eighteen knots. With a little extra effort she could do well over twenty, and frequently did, especially in the early days of the triangle run when she was in spirited competition with the fast steamers *Iroquois* and *Chippewa* of Joshua Green's American Pu-

2 As this is written, unconfirmed waterfront rumor has it that the two graceful three-stackers may not be ready for the scrapyard yet; that one may be converted to an Alaska cruise ship, the other to an automobile ferry.

Tees, above, was pioneer vessel of line founded in 1883 by Commodore John Irving, below.

get Sound Navigation Company,

The American steamers were fast boats in their own right in those days[3] but there is no record of either of them . . . or any other ship, for that matter . . . ever beating the *Princess Vic* in a fair race. In those golden days of the early twentieth century, CPR ran its coastal steamers with all the flair of Cunarders and the *Victoria's* crew included a handsomely uniformed trumpeter. His other duties were nebulous, but he became a heroic figure when, with black smoke boiling from her three smartly raked stacks, the *Princess Victoria* out-raced the *Iroquois* or *Chippewa*. Then he would stand on the *Princesse's* gracefull stern and blew derisive notes back at the hard-driven American steamers.

The Seattle *Times* of June 12, 1905 gave a vivid account of one of *Princess Vic's* early-day fast runs:

"The steamer *Princess Victoria* last evening on her run from Victoria to Seattle, broke the former record for speed, which was held by the same boat, by seven minutes time. The boat began speeding after backing away from the wharf at Victoria and turning her bow toward Seattle at exactly 6:59 o'clock. At the slow bell, given just as she was sliding up to the dock in Seattle, after a run of over seventy miles, the hands on the dial pointed at 10:16.

"A. B. Calder, general agent for the CPR in this city, made the statement that this was the fastest time ever made by any coast, sound or river boat in America. 'Should the *Empress of Japan*,' he continued, 'maintain such speed on her trip across the Pacific, she would reach Hong Kong in about nine days and two hours, thus lowering the speed record, which she already holds, by more than twenty-four hours.'

Occasionally some lesser craft failed to get out of the way of the fast stepping Princess and came to grief. In 1906 the little steamer *Chehalis* was run down and sunk by *Princess Vic* in Burrard Inlet with considerable loss of life. In 1908 she tangled with the halibut schooner *Ida May* on Puget Sound, but was able to push her badly punctured victim onto the beach before she sank. *Princess Vic's* most spectacular encounter occurred on the foggy morning of August 26, 1914, when she collided with the Pacific Alaska Navigation Company's *Admiral Sampson* off Point No Point on lower Puget Sound. The Admiral liner sank in minutes, with the loss of twelve lives.

3 Both the **Iroquois** and **Chippewa** are still in service (1959), the former as a freighter for Black Ball Transport Company, the latter as senior member of the Washington State ferry fleet on Puget Sound.

Princess Vic was, for the most part, a ladylike and well-behaved ship, however, and she logged better than three and a half million miles between 1903 and 1951, when she retired from passenger service and suffered the ignominious fate of being stripped down and converted to a hog-fuel barge. The beautiful speed queen of the Canadian coastal fleet was unable to adjust to her reduced circumstances. As the barge *Tahsis III*, she was loaded with hemlock pulp chips at Tahsis, Vancouver Island and, early in March, 1953, was led off by the nose toward Powell River by the tug *Sea Giant*. In Welcome Pass the aged Princess veered from her course, struck a rock and quickly sank. She had always come out on top in half a century's strandings and collisions, but ships, like people, become vulnerable when they are stripped of pride and dinity.

The *Princess Victoria* was joined, in 1908, by a graceful three-funneled running-mate, the *Princess Charlotte*, and the two set a standard of speed, luxury and good looks on the international triangle run. The three raked, buff and black stacks of the *Victoria* and *Charlotte* became virtual trademarks of this service, continued with the later handsome Princesses *Margaret, Irene, Marguerite* (1), *Elaine, Elizabeth* and *Joan*.

By the close of World War I the CPR coastal **stea**mers maintained ten routes with a fleet of twenty steamers. Its Alaska service from Victoria and Vancouver terminated at Skagway, with calls at Prince Rupert, Ketchikan, Wrangel and Juneau. The West Coast of Vancouver Island route, a rugged service handled for decades by the *Princess Maquinna*, provided connections with the outside world to 29 scattered settlements with such interesting names as Kyuquot Whaling Station, Quiet Cove, Clo-oose, Quatsino Cannery and Uchucklesit.

By 1959, with the last of the three-stackers, *Princess Elizabeth* and *Princess Joan*, withdrawn from service and awaiting the decision of CPR management as to scrapping or rejuvination, the company retains only one stateroom liner in service, the 317-foot *Princess Louise*. Built in 1921 and now used only as a summer cruise liner to Alaska, he days are certainly numbered.

The present-day CPR steamship service is largely a ferry operation, with the Vancouver-Nanaimo route as its backbone. Fortunately, the 6000-ton, two-funneled *Princess Patricia* (2) and *Princess Marguerite* (2), Glasgow-built

in 1949, still serve the traditional Seattle-Victoria-Vancouver triangle route during the summer months. While these handsome sisters are really only large day boats (they carry 2000 passengers, but have stateroom accommodations for only 98), they are thoroughly impressive. Furthermore, they're the nearest thing to the old-fashioned coastwise liner you're likely to see in this progressive and enlighted age.

PRINCESS VICTORIA, above, was noted for speed and beauty; Charmer, below, for frequent mishaps. Lower left is interior view of Princess Elizabeth taken shortly before she was withdrawn from service.

SHIPS OF THE C.P.R.

Left, top to bottom: **Princess Louise**, built in 1869 as **Olympia** was pioneer Puget Sound side-wheeler. In CPR service 1901-1906. **Otter**, built at Victoria, 1900. In service until 1931. **Beaver**, shown here in temporary trouble, was built in 1898, served CPN and CPR from 1901 to 1919. **Princess Victoria** of 1902, first CPR three-stacker, was Northwest speed queen.

Right, top to bottom: **Princess Charlotte** came from English yard 1908 as running mate for **Victoria**, is still in service in Europe. **Charmer**, built in 1887, was originally named **Premier.** Was involved in record number of shipwrecks and litigation. In service 1901-1935. **Princess Adelaide** came from Glasgow in 1910, was sold in 1949.

CANADIAN PACIFIC

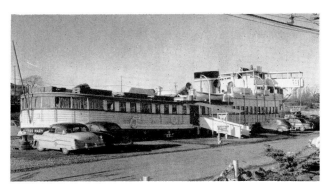

Left, top to bootom: **Princess Beatrice,** built in 1903 as first new CPR ship, remaining in service until 1928. **Princess Mary,** Esquimault-built in 1914, was retired in 1952, now serves as leading Victoria restaurant, operated by Island Tug and Barge Co. (lower photo)

Right, top to bottom: **Princess Ena,** steel freighter, came from Garston, England in 1907, was sold in 1931. **Princess Alice,** steel passenger and freight liner, was built at Newcastle in 1911, was sold in 1949. **Princess Royal,** built of wood at Esquimault in 1907, served British Columbia and Alaska routes until 1933.

SHIPS OF THE CPR

Left, top to bottom: **Princess Louise** (2) was built at Wallace Shipyards, North Vancouver, in 1921, remains in fleet as only Alaska cruise liner left in CPR service. **Princess Elaine** was built on the Clyde in 1928. **Princess Elizabeth**, Glasgow-built in 1930, served Seattle-Victoria-Vancouver triangle route until suspension of winter service in 1959. Her future is uncertain. **Princess Norah**, built at Glasgow in 1928 is now Alaska cruise liner **Queen of the North**. **Princess Joan**, 1930-built sister ship of **Elizabeth**, also ended winter triangle route service in winter of 1959; faces uncertain future. **Princess of Nanaimo**, built at Glasgow in 1950 and on Vancouver-Nanaimo shuttle service, proves that even a ferry can be a handsome ship.

CANADIAN PACIFIC

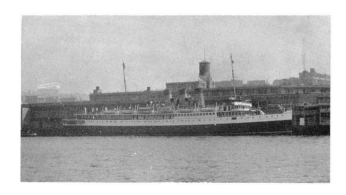

Left, top to bottom: **Princess May,** built at Newcastle in 1888, sailed under names **Cass, Arthur** and **Ningchow** before entering CPR service in 1901. Sold for Atlantic service in 1919. **Princess Kathleen,** sleek cruise liner of 1925 vintage met spectacular disaster in Alaskan waters in 1952. (page 187) **Princess Margaret** built at Dumbarton in 1914 was requisitioned for World War 1 service.

Right, top to bottom: **Princess Sophia,** built in Scotland in 1912, was victim of one of West Coast's worst marine disasters when she struck Vanderbilt Reef, Alaska in 1918 and went down with all hands. **Princess Maquinna,** built at Esquimault in 1913, served hazardous Vancouver Island west coast route for almost half century. **Princess Patricia** (2), and **Princess Marguerite** (2), are handsome twin ships built by Fairfield of Glasgow in 1949. Propelled by twin-screw turbo-electric engines of 15,500 horsepower, they cruise at 23 knots; handle triangle international route during summer months.

PRETTY PRINCESS Marguerite, shown leaving Seattle for Victoria, retains appearance of coastal liner, although she is primarily designed for passenger ferry duty on short runs. (She has accommodations for 2000 day passengers; stateroom space for only 98.)
Below, the ill-fated **Princess Sophia** is shown during World War 1 days while on a special excursion to Bellingham, Washington.

Princess Alice skirts majestic B.C. coast, above. Purser's
crew members of Princess Joan are shown below.

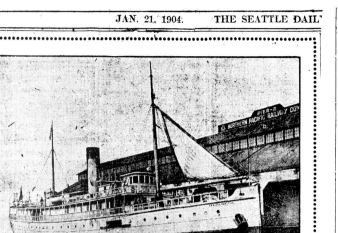

STEAMSHIP PRINCESS BEATRICE READY TO SAIL FROM SEATTLE DOCK

Canadian Pacific Railroad Company's fine new steamship left yesterday at 9.30 a. m. from Pier No. 2 on her first trip to Victoria. The vessel arrived here Monday night and was prepared for her maiden trip on the new run. She is scheduled to leave Seattle at 9:30 o'clock each morning, and returning, leave Victoria at 11 o'clock each night except Sunday. This makes it very convenient for all passengers coming from Tacoma and the valley points, so that they can leave home at a reasonable hour and take the boat for Victoria. She took a good list of passengers yesterday and the officials of the Canadian Pacific are much pleased at the start.

FAREWELL: The steamship Princess Elizabeth, long a familiar sight on the Seattle waterfront, pulled away from the Canadian Pacific Railway dock at the foot of Lenora Street yesterday on her final trip to Canada. C. P. R. is discontinuing winter service between Seattle, Victoria and Vancouver, B. C., and the Princess Joan and Princess Elizabeth are being retired permanently. The steamship company will resume summer service in mid-May, with the Princess Marguerite and Princess Patricia on the Seattle-Victoria-Vancouver run. Other vessels in Elliott Bay gave the departing passenger ship the traditional three-whistle salute.

year-round CPR steamer service; 1959 account tells of abandonment. Below, the **Princess Joan** whistles her last farewell to Seattle as she prepares to leave her pier for last winter run to Victoria.

UNION STEAM

Vancouver, British Columbia, home port of Union Steamships Ltd. for the past seventy years, is a great city whose own life span covers only a brief 73 years. Back in 1889, the infant town and the brand-new steamship company formed a lasting and useful partnership.

In the beginning Union Steamship Company Limited had a more imposing title than fleet list, for its largest vessel was the 76-foot tug *Skidgate*. Operating with this modest flagship mostly in harbor towing and on the old Moodyville-Hastings Mill ferry run, were the 57-foot paddle steamer *Leonora,* the 51-foot S.S. *Senator*, and a few small scows.

Determined to waste no time in expanding his company's activities to its avowed function of supplying the increased demand for freight and passenger service to the remote logging and fishing districts of the British Columbia coast, manager William Webster departed for England in search of new capital and new ships. There he joined forces with John Darling, former general superintendent of Union Steamship Company of New Zealand, who raised the needed funds and borrowed the familiar crimson, black-topped funnel markings of the older Union line for the new Canadian company. Arrangements were made for the Glasgow shipbuilding firm of Bow, McLachlan & Company to construct three steamers in sections, final assembly to be completed in British Columbia under the supervision of John Darling's son, Henry.

To supply the immediate needs of the company, Captain Webster journeyed on to India, where he purchased the S.S. *Cutch*, a 180-foot craft of 320 gross tons. Formerly the yacht of an Indian maharaja, the *Cutch* steamed under her own power and with Captain Webster in command from Bombay to Vancouver, arriving safely at her Carrall Street moorings in June of 1890. She was almost immediately placed in service hauling Canadian Pacific Railway passengers, mail and freight between Vancouver and Nanaimo, CPR not yet having entered the maritime field.

The three knocked-down ships from Glasgow arrived early the following year and their assembly began at a primitive shipyard hacked from the timber below present Stanley Park. The 101-foot *Comox*, first steel ship ever put together in British Columbia, was launched in October 1891. She became the company's first "logging steamer," serving the timber camps and isolated hand loggers along the upper British Columbia coast. The 120-foot *Capilano* followed the *Comox* in December, while the 127-foot steam schooner-type cargo steamer *Coquitlam* was launched in April, 1892.

Like American shipping companies, Union Steam suffered considerably in the depression years between 1893 and the Klondike rush of 1897. A venture into coastwise service between American and British Columbia ports during that period was almost disasterous. Two seagoing steamships, *Grandholm*[1] and *Tai Chow*, were chartered to transport CPR passengers and freight between the Columbia River and Vancouver by way of Victoria. Heavy financial losses resulting from this enterprise nearly bankrupted the struggling young steamship line.

Fate had another unkind blow in store for Union Steam during this pioneer era. The *Coquitlam*, serving as tender to the British Columbia sealing fleet in Alaska, was seized by United States authorities on a charge of illegally transferring cargo in American waters. The *Coquitlam* was eventually released on bond, but her cargo of seal skins was confiscated. The ensuing legal snarl was not entirely unravelled until 1921. Times were so hard that the company rented its warehouses for vegetable storage and kept the old *Leonora* busy hauling bargeloads of paving stone for Vancouver streets to help meet operating and legal expenses.

1 **Grandholm** was the ship which brought the three sectional ships **Capilano, Comox** and **Coquitlam** from Glasgow to Vancouver by way of Cape Horn.

STEAMING PAST FORESTED SHORES, Union Steam's *Chelohsin* presents a pretty and typical picture of British Columbia coastal shipping in its heyday. A twin-screw steel steamer, *Chelohsin* served Union Steam from her launching in 1911 until her fatal stranding at Vancouver in 1949.

Things changed fast after July of 1897. *Capilano* was the first British vessel to join the gold rush, departing for Nome with the stern-wheeler *Lightning* in tow. The *Coquitlam* soon joined her, the two little steamers shuttling busily back and forth between Vancouver and the Alaskan gold rush ports for the next two years. *Cutch* entered the Skagway trade in 1898, remaining on the run until her stranding on Horseshoe Reef near Juneau in 1900.

The gold rush had, by then, become more orderly and less frenzied, with the Seattle-Skagway liners handling the bulk of the Alaska trade. The rapid expansion of the logging and fishing industries along the British Columbia coast more than took up the slack, however, with the *Comox* and the new *Cassiar* busily engaged in that service. By 1904 business had improved to such an extent that a first-class coastal passenger and freight steamer, the *Camosun,* was built for the company in Scotland. The *Camosun,* a 192-foot steel vessel of 1,400 tons made the voyage to Vancouver under her own steam, by way of the Straits of Magellan. The *Camosun* was placed on the Vancouver-Prince Rupert run in expectation of the completion of the Grand Trunk Pacific Railway to its western tidewater terminal at Prince Rupert.

The railway company brought with it its own steamship line to compete with the Canadian Pacific and Union Steam fleets for the British Columbia coastal trade, but Union Steam, financially backed by the Prince Rupert

THE SNOW'S THE SAME, although the upper photograph was taken at Skagway during gold rush days, the lower one in 1947. The old-timer above is the **Cutch,** which worked for Union Steam from 1890 to 1900; later became the Colombian gunboat **Bogota.** The sleek little liner **below** is the **Coquitlam** (2), now the Alaska cruise ship **Glacier Queen** of Alaska Cruise Lines Ltd.

SHIPS OF THE UNION STEAM

Left, top to bottom: **Cutch**, former yacht of Indian prince was Union's first full-size ship. Built in 1884, she earned gold rush profits for young company. **Comox**, first new Union ship in 1891, was sold for scrap in 1919. **Capilano**, also launched in 1891, was wrecked on B.C. coast in 1914. **Cassair** of 1890 was in Union service from 1901 to 1923, when she was sold and converted to floating cannery under her original name of **J. R. McDonald**. Burned, 1940.

Right, top to bottom: **Camosun**, first Canadian coaster to be equipped with wireless, was built in 1905; lasted until 1936, when she was scrapped. **Cowichan**, launched in 1908 as **Caribou**, was sunk in collision with line's **Lady Cynthia** in 1925. **Cheakamus** served as naval tug in World War 2; was scrapped shortly thereafter.

SHIPS OF THE UNION STEAM

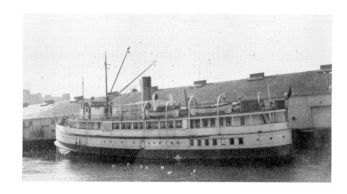

Left, top to bottom: **Capilano** (2) was a 1946-built freighter operated by Union from 1951 until close of business in 1959. **Brittania** was purchased with Terminal Steam Navigation Co. of Capt. J. A. Cates. **Cardena**, twin-screw steel steamer built in 1923; now in layup. **Skidgate**, 1879-vintage steam tug, was one of original three-boat union fleet of 1889. Scrapped in 1900. **Tees**, CPR old-timer, was operated briefly by Union Steam. **Chelohsin** was 1100-ton steel passenger carrier. **Catala**, twin-screw, two-stacker was in fleet from 1925 to 1957.

LADY ALEXANDRA, above, was one of Union Steam's handsome fleet of day boats, while Chilcotin, lower left, was one of three converted World War 2 corvettes used in post-war coastal passenger and freight service. Ships of this class are still operated on summer cruise service to Alaska by Alaska Cruise Lines (lower right).

SHIPS OF UNION STEAM

Left, top to bottom: **Camosun (2), ex-Prince Charles,** was built in 1907, was operated by Union from 1940 to 1945, when she was sold and renamed **Cairo.** Scrapped, 1952. **Lady Cynthia,** World War 1 minesweeper, was converted to day liner in 1925, sold and scrapped in 1957. **Lady Cecilia,** also a 1919 minesweeper, was cut down to barge in 1951.

Right, top to bottom: **Lady Alexandra** was built in 1924, retired in 1952. **Chilcotin** on Alaska cruise. **Camosun (3),** was also 1943-built Royal Canadian Navy corvette before 1946 conversion to passenger-freight liner. **Coquitlam,** ex-HMCS **Hespeler,** is now the summer cruise liner **Glacier Queen.**

mail contract, soon had the Scottish-built *Co-wichan* on the run with the *Camosun*.

By World War I, the Union fleet was well entrenched in the British Columbia coastal service and was preparing to enter the short-run excursion business. Purchase of the All Red Line, which had maintained a two-ship service between Vancouver and Powell River, included Selma Park, a favorite excursion area near Vancouver. Three years later Union Steam purchased the Terminal Steam Navigation Company of Captain J. A. Cates, together with that company's popular Bowen Island resort. The eventual result was the addition to the Union roster of a fleet of handsome *Lady* class day liners designed exclusively for the local excursion trade. The first of these, *Lady Alexandra*, arrived from Scotland in 1924. The *Lady Cecilia* and *Lady Cynthia* arrived the following year. In addition to the day runs and cargo sailings, Union Steam operated three weekly sailings to Prince Rupert, Anyox, Skeena River and Bella Coola, three logging camp runs and two local runs to Sechelt, Powell River and Howe Sound ports.

Service was further expanded after World War II with the conversion of three British Castle class corvettes into the sleek passenger-cargo liners *Chilcotin, Coquitlam* and *Camosun* which reestablished passenger service by Union steamers as far north as Skagway. The pretty trio arrived on the scene at the close of an era, however, for the day of the regularly scheduled coastal passenger liner was ending. It was the same depressing story of constantly rising operating costs and airline competition for the first-class passenger business.

The March, 1958 issue of *Steamboat Bill of Facts,* quarterly publication of the Steamship Historical Society of America, carried the following obituary to Union Steam passenger operations, written by Lloyd M. Stadum, well known Northwest marine historian:

"The long-dreaded recent announcement of the withdrawal of Union Steamships' passenger fleet breaks a service that has existed continuously since 1889 * * * since that time the smart, black-hulled vessels, with their red and black-topped stacks, have served nearly every port along the rugged coast of British Columbia. They have also traded to Alaska and made many trips into Puget Sound waters."

Shortly thereafter the modern passenger liners *Camosun* and *Coquitlam* were sold to Alaska Cruise Lines, headed by Charles B. West of Seattle, and placed in summer-only cruise

service between Vancouver and Skagway. During the 1958 season they were manned and victualled by Union Steamships. During the summer of 1959 they are scheduled to operate from the Canadian National pier, with crews supplied by C.N.

On January 25 the *Marine Digest* reported, "All the floating assets of Union Steamships Ltd., British Columbia's oldest shipping company, have been sold to the Northland Navigation Company Ltd. The sale ends an historic maritime link in B.C. commerce."

It was the close of another era.

Northland Navigation Company, successor to historic Union Steam, was founded by Australian-born Capt. H. J. C. Terry in 1943 as the British Columbia Steamship Company Ltd., operating the small coastal freighter *Alaska Prince*. The firm adopted its present name in 1954. In addition to the remaining Union passenger vessels, the firm operates the former Canadian Pacific ships *Queen of the North* (ex-*Princess Norah*) and *Princess of Alberni*. Under Northland ownership, the old CPR steamers have been renamed *Canadian Prince* and *Nootka Prince*.

For the 1959 season Northland Navigation Company announced continuation of year-round service on some of the historic routes formerly served by Union Steam. *Catala* operates a twice-weekly service to Rivers Inlet, Bella Coola, Port Hardy and way points. Weekly service to the Queen Charlotte Islands is provided by *Cassiar* and *Chilliwack*, while S.S. *Canadian Prince* serves Alert Bay, Bella Coola, Butedal and Prince Rupert, connecting at Alert Bay with M.S. *Lady Rose,* providing ferry service to Sointula, Port McNeill, Harbledown Island and Telegraph Cove. M.S. *Alaska Prince* handles freight and passengers as far north as Prince Rupert, while *Canadian Prince* will extend her run to Stewart and Hyder, Alaska, during the summer months.

Up for sale, and probably destined for the shipbreaker's yard, are such veteran Union coastal liners as *Cardena, Chenega* and *Lady Alexandra.*

GRAND TRUNK PACIFIC

For many years after the completion of Canadian Pacific's transcontinental railway, capitalists had given thought to a rival line designed to cut itself in on the vast undeveloped potential of western Canada as well as the tidy profits already being enjoyed by the single existing line. It was not until October 24, 1903, however, that anything concrete was done about it. On that date the Grand Trunk Pacific Railway was chartered for the purpose of constructing a second transcontinental railway across Canada. Prince Rupert was selected as western terminus for the new road.

Although actual construction began in 1906, the manifold problems of blasting a roadbed and laying steel through the rugged terraine of Northern Canada made for slow going. The still unfinished road received a tragic setback when, in April of 1912, its president, Charles M. Hays, went down with the White Star liner *Titanic*.

Although the first through passenger train was not destined to arrive at Prince Rupert until April 9, 1914, the line's organizers were both optimistic and ambitious. Aware that Canadian Pacific's fine fleet of coastal steamships was a vital factor in funneling passengers to the CPR rail terminus at Vancouver, Grand Trunk Pacific officials were determined not be outdone in the realm of maritime speed and luxury. The new Grand Trunk steamships arrived on the Pacific Coast long before its first train chugged across the Fraser River and whistled into Prince Rupert.

The Seattle *Times* of June 11, 1910 enthusiastically reported on the arrival of the first of them:

"With her hull and bulwarks gleaming like ivory in the fitful sunshine, the new Grand Trunk Pacific liner *Prince Rupert,* from Newcastle-on-Tyne, drew into her slip at the foot of Madison Street this morning while vessels in the harbor shrieked a true Seattle welcome to the officers and men aboard.

"Probably no vessel which has arrived in Elliott Bay in years was the subject of so much favorable comment from seafaring men. As soon as the vessel was tied up, an informal reception, to which the general public had been invited, was held aboard. Resident engineer Fred T. Lucas of the Grand Trunk Pacific Dock Company and Matthew Dow, contractor building the new dock, were warmly congratulated on having wharf and buildings erected in time to accommodate the new steamer. The receptions will continue until 10 o'clock tonight.

"The *Prince Rupert* started from Victoria on the last leg of her long voyage from England to Seattle at 4 o'clock this morning and, proceeding under a slow bell, reached her destination at 9 o'clock. Captain Johnson took command of the vessel June 6 from Captain A. M. Davis, who brought her from Newcastle to Victoria. Capt. Davis says that she is a remarkably fine seagoing vessel. On her trial trip, fully laden, she averaged eighteen and three-quarters knots and her commercial speed will equal sixteen knots. Since reaching Victoria, the *Prince Rupert* has been to Boat Harbor, where she coaled; on the drydock at Esquimault, and at Vancouver. At Vancouver and Victoria the *Prince Rupert* was thrown open for inspection and was visited by thousands of persons.

"The *Prince Rupert* is a twin-screw steamer and will go on the route from Seattle to Vancouver, calling at Victoria and Prince Rupert. She will start on her first trip Sunday midnight. Like the twin vessel, *Prince George,* which is due to arrive here next month, the *Prince Rupert* is rigged after the fashion of a two-mast fore-and-aft schooner, with three smokestacks, straight stem and cruiser stern.

"On the shelter and shade decks are long steel houses giving spacious accommodations for first-class passengers, together with the elaborate and tastefully decorated public rooms which are a special feature of the vessel. The upper deck house is designed to give ample promenade walk at the sides and around the ship. The hull is designed with remarkably fine

lines forward and a clear run aft to obtain a high speed commensurate with the power of the engines.

"Her length over all is 320 feet; breadth, exreme, 43¾ feet; gross tonnage 3,380 tons, deadweight carrying capacity, 1,100 tons; water ballast 606 tons. She is equipped with twin-screw engines, triple expansion with four cylinders and cranks balanced on the Yarrow, Schlick and Tweedy system to insure smooth running without vibration. Her indicated horse-power is 6000.

"She has two large double-ended and two large single-ended boilers of 180 pounds working pressure, Howden's forced draught. Her speed is eighteen and one-half knots, loaded. Passenger accommodations are, 220 first class, 132 second class and she has promenade space for about 1,500 excursionists."

The *Prince Rupert's* sister-liner, *Prince George,* arrived at Seattle on July 21, 1910, receiving a similar noisy welcome. On Decem-

ber 18 of that year the *Prince George* made double headlines, first by "running from Vancouver to Prince Rupert in thirty hours, most of the time at a speed of more than eighteen knots, a record for a commercial steamship without precedent in this part of the world."

Upon completing this notable voyage, the *Prince George* made further news by running herself ignominiously ashore in the first narrows at the entrance to Vancouver harbor. The receding tide left her high and dry, but she survived until September, 1954, when she grounded on rocks near Ketchikan in a heavy fog. One of her fuel ttnks exploded and the big steamer was gutted by fire. Although her 50 passengers were safely removed by Coast Guard and Army vessels, the *Prince George* was a total loss. The *Prince Rupert* survived her handsome sister by two years; then, in 1956 was sold to Japanese owners for scrapping.

The ornate Grank Trunk dock in Seattle was also almost destroyed by fire in later years. Its remnants, shorn of imposing clock tower and glass-windowed waiting rooms, still stands at the foot of Madison Street, occupied by Black Ball Freight Service, but it has become a work-aday structure which doesn't distract the interest of tourists from the big red city fireboats and Ivar's legendary Acres of Claims seafood restaurant next door.

Heavy construction costs and World War I losses doomed the ambitious Grand Trunk Pacific to financial limbo. Taken over by the Canadian government in 1920, the line has continued in operation as a unit of Canadian National Railways. The Seattle run was discontinued, with the steamers operating only between Vancouver and Prince Rupert, and on summer excursions to Alaska.

Under nationalized management the line, in 1930, added the modern steamers *Prince Robert, Prince Henry* and *Prince David* to its fleet, but like all the coastwise steamship lines, the close of World War II and the growth of airline competition spelled the doom of profitable operations.

As this is written the modern counterpart of the old Grand Trunk Pacific retains only the handsome twin-screw 350-footer *Prince George,* and she operates only during the summer months on excursion runs between Vancouver and Skagway. The company also operates the former Union Steam liners *Yukon Star* and *Glacier Queen* in the same service as agents for Alaska Cruise Lines Ltd.

Prince George, top, and Prince Rupert, lower.

Like other northern cruise liners, Grand Trunk steamers took tourists to the showplaces of southern Alaska. The **Prince Rupert** is pictured here, in typical Inside Passage settings.

ADDING SMOKE AND STEAM to Northern mists, the second Prince George, wearing Canadian National colors, works her way up the British Columbia coast, above. She's the only passenger liner still operated by Canadian National. Prince Henry, below, a product of the 1930's, was recently sold to foreign owners.

Views of **Prince David** contrast with tall-stacked **Prince Rupert,** center.

NORTHLAND TRANSPORTATION COMPANY, comparatively short-lived though it was, operated a number of fine ships between Seattle and Alaska from its formation in the early 1920's until its post-war merger with Alaska Steam. Organized by the Sunny Point Canning Company with the old **Bellingham,** the little motorship **Northland,** right center, was soon added to the fleet. Trim steamers like the **North Sea,** top, and **North Coast,** lower right, came later. Lower left, Inside Passage from the **North Sea.**

North Coast, above, night loading at Seattle. North Sea, below, discharges freight and passengers at Sitka.

ALASKA TRANSPORTATION COMPANY, another small
independent line, operated from 1935 to 1948, growing from
small wooden ships like **Tongass** (ex-**Wapama**), to the big
George Washington, shown above in drydock.

TYEE, CRUISING INSIDE PASSAGE, above, and **Taku**
were handsome little steamships, formerly in the fruit
trade, which became workhorses of Alaska Transportation
Company's freight and passenger trade.

The mellow blast of their whistles, (that's **Taku's** on the
right) called many travelers to far northern journeys in
the company's brief period of activity.

FORMER NEW YORK TO BERMUDA CRUISE LINER George Washington, above, had brief career on West Coast. She arrived in Seattle on February 9, 1948, but ATC was out of business before the year was over. Last of the fleet to remain on the West Coast was the steam schooner **Tongass**, lower left, which lay rotting in Lake Union for ten years until, in 1959, she was towed south to be restored to her glory days as the **Wapama** for exhibit at San Francisco Marine Museum. **Zapora**, former fishing steamer, lower right, was an original unit of ATC fleet.

GRAND OLD LADY

It's hard to realize that Old Vic is gone from the Pacific Northwest seaways, although the Grand Old Lady made her last voyage from those familiar waters back in August, 1956. Then, as the lowly barge *Straits Maru*, she was dragged off across the Pacific for scrapping in Japan.

It was a sad end for a great ship famed, until her reduction to a barge in 1954, as the oldest active vessel in the American Merchant Marine.

The venerable ship, launched in 1870 as the Cunard Line's *Parthia*, made her last offshore voyage in the summer of 1952. During the years between she worked most of the world's sea lanes under the British and American flags, served in four wars and a filibustering expedition, and gained fame as an Alaskan treasure ship.

The *Victoria* was built for the Cunard Line by W. Denny & Bros. at Dumbarton, Scotland, and was launched as the *Parthia*. Designed for the low-cost emigrant trade between Ireland and the United States, she was built for economy rather than speed and luxury, but there was no penny-pinching in the construction of her sturdy hull. Her subsequent long and adventurous life amply proved that.

During her 15 years of service as a Cunard liner on the North Atlantic the little iron ship was as much windjammer as steamship. She was fitted with an 1800-horsepower compound engine, but she was also fully rigged as a three-masted bark and her canvas wasn't carried just for decorative effect. When blessed with favorable winds, her engine was disconnected from the shaft, the screw was feathered, and she ramped across the Atlantic under sail only. It saved a lot of coal for the Cunard Line and the passengers probably enjoyed it.

The *Parthia* went to war for the first time in 1881, serving as a British trooper in the Egyptian campaign. Four years later Cunard turned her over to John Elder & Company as part of the down payment on the new liners *Umbria* and *Etruria*. At that time she was re-engined with the triple-expansion steam plant that served her until 1954. After that she was placed on a run to Australia, the Hebrides and South America.

The Canadian Pacific Railway Company took her over in 1887 and transferred her to the West Coast. She operated in that company's Vancouver-Orient service until 1891, when the famed clipper-bowed Empress liners replaced her. Then she went back to England for another overhaul and was renamed *Victoria* just before she returned to the Pacific in 1892. Another change of owners that year put her on the run between Tacoma and the Orient, flying the house flag of Dodwell & Company's North Pacific Steamship Company. In this service her fleetmates were two other former British liners, the *Olympia* and the *Tacoma*.

Although she was known primarily as an Orient liner in those days, she took time out to make three voyages as a United States Army troopship during the war with Spain, and also to journey to Nome during the height of the Alaskan gold rush.

In 1903 Old Vic was taken over by the Northwestern Steamship Company. Later, when war broke out between Japan and Russia, she became a blockade runner along with the *Tacoma* and the *Olympia*. Loaded with supplies for the beleagured Russians at Vladivostok, the three steamers headed out from Seattle to play their dangerous game with the Japanese navy.

The *Olympia's* crown sheet burned out and killed one of her engineers, and she had to limp back to Seattle, where her cargo was sold. The *Tacoma*, captured by Japanese warships, became a prize of war. Only the *Victoria* came through the adventure unscathed.

Victoria as Cunard Liner **Parthia** of 1870.

The Guggenheim interests gained control of what was left of the Northwestern fleet shortly after its ill-starred filibustering expedition, and the *Victoria,* became a full-time Alaska liner. When the line was merged with the Alaska Steamship Company in 1908, the *Victoria* hoisted the Black Ball flag as part of the expanded fleet.

Old Vic had proved during the earlier gold rush days that her sturdy iron hull made her well suited to the far northern routes. She continued to prove it every spring, for she was usually the first ship to plow through the melting ice of the Nome roadstead when navigation opened. She was often the last ship out in the late autumn, too, and frequently had to hurry. In addition to the danger of being frozen in for the winter, she was faced by the fact that her insurance premiums sky-rocketed to astronomical heights if she happened to be caught in the Bering Sea after November 1.

Even when there was no emergency, Old Vic did a lot of racing during her passenger-carrying days in the Far North. She had never been noted as a speed queen on the Atlantic, but with her triple-expansion engines and fine lines she was able to outrun most of her rivals on the

Pacific. She made the most of it. In November 1909 Seattle newspapers reported that she was racing the rival Pacific Coast Steamship Company liner *Senator* down from Nome.

Smashing through violent storms all the way, Old Vic soon overhauled the *Senator,* which had left Nome 25 hours ahead of her, and arrived at Seattle a full day before her rival.

She later staged memorable races with the liner *Ohio,* but few of her rivals lasted long on the hazardous northern sea lane. The *Senator* and the *Ohio* fell victims of reefs and hidden rocks. So did the *Victoria's* old fleetmate *Olympia,* but the old champion seldom faltered. Throughout her career she was a remarkably lucky ship. Even on the Alaska run, a ships' graveyard if ever there was one, she suffered only two accidents of any consequence.

In 1907 the Old Vic struck an iceberg near Nome, filling her No. 2 hold almost to the main deck, but her bulkheads held and she made it to Seattle for repairs. Three years later she hit the beach at the foot of Hinchinbrook Island on the Inside Passage, but she was refloated with no permanent scars.

Many Alaska travelers attributed the Old Vic's amazing safety record to some sort of

STILL EQUIPPED WITH SAILS, Victoria was in trans-
pacific service when this early photograph was taken at
Victoria, British Columbia.
Next page: Victoria in the ice.

Capt. Frank Huxtable and Chief Purser Wilbur Thompson
on the S.S. North Sea.

supernatural protection that gave her a charmed
life. Others credited her long-time master,
Capt. John (Dynamite) O'Brien. But all agreed
that it was wise to travel on the *Victoria* if you
wanted to be sure of getting where you were
going. Ship after ship piled on the hidden rocks
or ripped themselves open on the floating ice
of the fog-shrouded, storm-ridden northern
seas, but Old Vic always came through.

Capt. Dynamite John, almost as famous as
his ship in Northwest marine annals, was a
classic Irish shellback and a fitting commander
for the colorful Old Vic. Born in Cork in 1848,
he served as apprentice in British full-rigged
ships and managed to cover most of the globe
before reaching Seattle. On one voyage across
the Pacific he cracked on all sail in an effort to
get his dying owner from Hawaii to the States
to fulfill his last wish. He wanted to be buried
in American soil.

Death caught up with the racing schooner,
however, and Captain John's boss, who was his
friend as well, was taken at sea many days out
from the Columbia River. But the skipper had
made a promise and he meant to keep it.

The ship carried an assortment of spices in
her cargo. Somewhere Captain John had read
about ancient Egyptian embalming methods.
Those were the days when a sea captain had

VICORTIA's massive hull of wrought iron coupled with her powerful engines made her a trailblazer on the sea road to Nome for many years. She shouldered her way through ice floes that were impassable to lesser ships, was thus able to make early season runs to the far north. She was also frequently the last ship to sail for Stateside ports from the Yukon's mouth.

In this pre-World War I photograph the Grand Old Lady is shown steaming through Bering Sea ice floes close to her journey's end at Nome Roadstead.

to be ready to try his hand at almost anything in an emergency, so the skipper saw nothing unusual in this last service he was called upon to render his owner. The perfectly embalmed body of the dead shipowner was carried to port by Captain John for burial in American soil.

When Captain John was on the beach in the summer of 1931, laid up by the illness from which he was never to recover, he got a letter from the passengers who were sailing north on the *Victoria*. It summed up how he was regarded by those who sailed the northern sea lanes:

"As we sail away to the Northland, we want you to know that we are wishing the best of everything for an old friend and the best skipper who ever sailed Alaskan waters."

Captain John was dying, but he was strong enough to write an answer before the Old Vic sailed. In it he said, "My old command, the *Victoria*, will see you safely to the land of eternal friendships. I will be on hand to greet you when you return."

The *Victoria's* master wasn't there to meet his ship when she raced the ice down from Nome at season's end, but those who sailed with him haven't forgotten him.

Old Vic continued to sail as an Alaska passenger liner until 1937. At the end of that season she was retired, but not for long. When the clouds of another war began to gather in 1940, she was converted into a freighter and returned to her old run. In Navy gray, mounting guns fore and aft, she served the northern outposts throughout the war, a war in which her old fleetmate *Northwestern* was bombed by Japanese planes at Dutch Harbor, Alaska.

When the war ended she continued in service, making the northern freight runs during the peak of the summer season. When she steamed south at the close of her last voyage in 1952 she was still a fine, trim ship. Her great

hull of hand-wrought Swedish iron was as sturdy as in 1870. Her engine, built by John Elder in 1885, was still smooth and powerful. She could still steam at 13 knots, and her crews loved her, for she handled beautifully, like the grand old lady she was. Old Vic was as steady and comfortable as any ship afloat.

But progress had caught up with the old sea queen at last. The Alaska Steamship Company was shipping freight north in new-fangled unitized containers, and Old Vic's small holds wouldn't accommodate the big packages. The end of the Korean war released modern coastal motorships much cheaper to operate. The *Victoria* was finished as a steamer.

The old ship, however, was found to be "in beautiful shape" while on the dock for inspection. Stripped of her engines and upperworks, she joined the Straits Towing fleet of 36 steam and diesel tugs and 65 barges in a coastwise trade which extends from Alaska to Mexico.

Finally, her days of usefulness ended, even as a barge, the slim iron hull was loaded with scrap iron and towed to Japan by Straits Towing Company's giant sea-going tug *Sudbury*.

The Queen is dead at last.

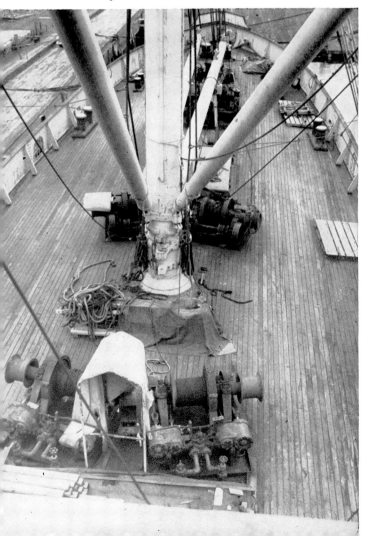

LONG CAREER: Opposite page, top, Old Vic in Bering Sea ice with revenue cutter **Bear.** Next she's shown leaving Nome on November 12, 1916, latest departure ever made, then as armed World War 2 freighter, being towed away for dismantling as a barge and, finally, on her last voyage, towed by Canadian tug **Sudbury,** for scrapping in Japan.

Views on this page were taken by Puget Sound Maritime Historical Society members on farewell visit to **Victoria** just before she was dismantled.

Bar, above, and dining salon of S.S. **Victoria.**

NORTHERN SHIPWRECK

The sun has set, and all alone
The steamer battles with the sea;
Her plume of smoke is backward blown,
Beneath her prow, with bodeful moan,
The conquering wave bends sullenly.
And chill and drear, a shadow creeps
Along the wild and misty deeps
That roll to windward and a-lee.

...The Wreck of the Wright
by Samuel L. Simpson

It was the custom, in nineteenth century America, to properly memorialize any sea disaster worthy of note with funereal poetry like that above, written back in 1873 by one of the Pacific Coast's earliest poets to mark the mysterious passing of the trim little steamship *George S. Wright*.

The *Wright* was launched from the Port Ludlow shipyard in 1863 for pioneer shipping man John T. Wright, who named her for his brother. Later taken over by the North Pacific Transportation Company, she was one of the first vessels to operate between Portland and Alaska ports.

Ten years after her launching, the *Wright* put out from Sitka headed south for Nanaimo. She never made port. Weeks after her disappearance a few bits of wreckage and two bodies were found on the beach near Cape Caution and it was assumed that she had struck an uncharted rock in that vicinity and gone down with all hands.

Some excitement was created when an Indian, arrested for drunken and licentious behavior on the staid streets of Victoria, gave forth with a blood-curdling story about the *Wright's* passengers and crew having reached shore safely, where they were forthwith butchered by hostile Indians. No proof of this accusation was ever found, but the exact fate of the *George S. Wright* and her ship's company remains a mystery to this day.

The loss of the *George S. Wright* was not the first shipwreck on the Inside Passage of Alaska . . . Captain Vancouver's exploration ships *Discovery* and *Chatham* were both stranded temporarily there in 1792 . . . nor was it by any means the last. The toll of lost ships in Alaskan waters is long and grim enough to provide whole volumes of lugubrious verse.

The thousand-mile Inside Passage, stretching from Seattle to Skagway, is almost a continuation of that great inland sea of the Northwest, Puget Sound, its seaward flank protected by hundreds of islands, great and small. It is, however, cursed with clinging fogs and blinding snow storms. Icebergs, spawned by the northern glaciers, stalk its narrow channels like deadly ghosts and thousands of jagged pinnacle rocks and sunken reefs add to its hazards.

Not a single lighthouse was built in Alaskan waters until 1902, while drag surveys designed to find and chart the under-sea hazards of rocks and reefs were not begun until World War I days. The mortality rate of northern ships has been so high, on this waterway alone, that a full history of the subject would fill many books this size.

The Alaska Gold Rush of 1897 brought maritime disaster in the Far North to a new high. The glittering treasure of the Klondike had not only brought prosperity to the Pacific Coast; it had brought a new lease on life to scores of worn-out hulks, many of which had been resting drearily on mudflats and in marine bone-yards for years. Strengthened with paint, putty and good intentions, they were advertised as "fast and palatial ocean-going steamships," had all the passengers and freight they could hold crammed aboard, and set off to face the manifold dangers of one of the world's most dangerous sea lanes. A great many of them fell by the wayside.

One such was the steam schooner *Clara Nevada*; home port, Portland, Oregon. This ancient iron steamer had given the best years of her life to the United States Government as the survey ship *Hassler*. Having been condemned and sold out of government service, she found herself, in her decrepit old age, hauling capacity loads of freight and passengers to Skagway and Dyea, starting points for the overland trek to the gold fields of the Yukon.

She left Dyea on the bleak and stormy night of February 5, 1898, headed south with a crew of 28 and a passenger list estimated at about sixty-five. Like the *George S. Wright,* a quarter of a century earlier, the *Clara Nevada* just never showed up anywhere. Shore-dwellers along Berner's Bay, south of Dyea, reported seeing and hearing an explosion out on the stormy waters of the bay the night of the steamer's disappearance, but it was not until fishermen pulled the ship's charred name-board and the burned body of her purser from the sea that any real clue of her fate was established.

The loss of the *Clara Nevada* was soon forgotten, for other Gold Rush ships met disaster . . . fifteen of them in that year of 1898 alone. None of the others, however, provided such a spine-chilling epilogue as did the *Clara Nevada*. It was in 1908 . . . ten years, almost to the day, from the time of her loss, and upon just such a storm-lashed night . . . that she came back.

Keepers of the Elder Rock light in Lynn Canal huddled near the stove in their quarters, listening to the storm's fury grinding great boulders together in the sea's bed under their feet. The storm found the ghost of the ancient, long-dead *Clara Nevada,* too, lifted her from the bottom of the sea and sent her riding the dark waters of Lynn Canal again.

In the morning the lighthouse keepers found the barnacled, weed-draped corpse of the *Clara Nevada,* dead and buried a full decade, high and dry on the south point of Elder Island. She had brought the bones of her long-vanished company with her and they found Christian burial, at least, in a common grave ashore.

Many of the old Alaska liners seemed to live charmed lives, making their hazardous voyages year after year without suffering fatal mishap, but the law of averages usually caught up with the best of them. The fabled Alaska treasure ship *Portland* was typical of the proverbially lucky ones whose luck ran out at last.

Built for the Hayti (as Haiti was then spelled) Mail Steamship Company by the New England Shipbuilding Company, of Bath, Maine, she was a wooden two-decker, 191.5 feet long, her single screw driven by a compound reciprocating steam engine. Under her original name, *Haytien Republic,* she wasted little time in developing a reputation as something of a maritime black sheep.

GOLD SHIP PORTLAND had many temporary strandings, like the one pictured at the left, but she never sailed again after striking an uncharted reef off Katala in 1910 (right).

— WRECK OF THE "SADIE" CAPE YORK, ALASKA —

NORTHERN COMMERCIAL COMPANY'S SIDE-WHEEL STEAMER SADIE was a brand new steel oil-burner in 1904, when she sailed north to operate out of Nome, but before the year was over she presented the sad picture shown above, driven ashore near Cape York by a sudden Arctic gale and abandoned to the ice and snow.

Three years after her 1885 lauching she became involved in the Hippolyte Rebellion in the island republic for which she was named. Charged with smuggling in brass cannon to the rebels, she was seized by the government and her boiler manhole covers impounded at the post office.

Thus immobilized, the *Haytien Republic* fell victim to an autumn storm in the harbor of Saint Marc; was blown violently onto a reef. Eventually she was rescued by the United States cruisers *Galena* and *Yantic*. Haytien president Legitime did not surrender gracefully, however. Before the *Haytien Republic* could depart from the harbor he sent out the transport *Nouvelle Velorogus* to express his displeasure by violently butting the poor *Haytien Republic,* leaving her further bruised and dented.

Having become *persona non grata* in Hayti, the steamer eventually made her way around the Horn to San Francisco where, in 1889, she was placed in competition with the Pacific Coast Steamship Company on the San Francisco-Seattle run, a service in which she lost large amounts of money for her owners, Getz Brothers & Company of San Francisco.

U.S.S. HASSLER, below, provided grim ghost story of the sea in her old age as Clara Nevada.

S.S. ISLANDER, as crack flagship of Canadian Pacific fleet, above, and as rotted derelict 33 years later, below.

CITY OF SEATTLE lost her propeller in 1905, had to beach herself near Petersburg.

Following a forlorn interval in the boneyard, the *Haytien Republic* was sold to the Merchants Steamship Company of Portland for the Columbia River-Vancouver-Puget Sound service. Caught smuggling Chinese from Canada to the United States, the old filibuster was impounded and sold by the U.S. Marshal for the humiliating sum of sixteen thousand dollars. It was at this time, in 1893, that her name was changed to *Portland,* probably in an effort to cover up her unsavory past. For some time the Pacific Coast people ran her, under charter, to various Central American ports, but in 1897 she was chartered by the North American Trading & Transportation Company . . . just in time to earn a legitimate place in history as the legendary treasure ship of the Yukon.

As is often the case, good publicity brought prosperity with it. The *Portland,* now looked upon as a fabulously lucky ship, was booked solid for every voyage to the north. It appeared that her reputation was justified, for she experienced numerous hairbreadth escapes from disaster. When caught in the ice with the *Jeanie* in 1902, the *Portland* was carried six hundred miles into the Arctic north of St. Michael, but she broke out at last and made it safely back to her destination.

In 1903 and 1904 she was again caught by the Arctic ice pack; again bucked her way out. In 1905 she ran full tilt into Spire Island, near Ketchikan, a mishap which required $25,000-worth of drydock surgery, but confounded Capt. L. J. Schage of the *Santa Clara,* who had seen the *Portland* on her rocky perch and reported in Seattle that she was, without doubt, a total loss.

Taken over in 1906 by H. F. Alexander's Alaska Coast Company, the old *Portland* celebrated the event by ramming herself onto some rocks on Entrance Island, near Nanaimo, with such force that her foremast broke off and, although Capt. Philip Mason managed to work her off, she was leaking so badly that she had to be beached again on Gabriola Island.

Again she was rescued to resume her headline-making career, but the remarkable luck of the *Portland* ran out completely on November 12, 1910, when she draped herself across an uncharted reef near Katalla. Capt. Franz Moore got her off and ran her full speed onto the nearby breach, where her passengers and crew, along with the U.S. Mail, were safely removed, but the famous old ship was finished. Wreckers stripped her of all her useful fittings, after which she was abandoned to slowly fall apart on that grim northern beach.

The *Portland's* reputation as a lucky ship was maintained to the end, however, for none of her people were ever killed or seriously injured in the course of her accident-prone career. Fate did not always deal so kindly with those who rode the northern liners.

It was on the evening of August 14, 1901 that the handsome Canadian Pacific Navigation Company steamship *Islander*, carrying one of the heaviest passenger loads since the height of the gold rush, swung away from the Skagway wharf and headed south toward Juneau and Victoria. It was, perhaps, at about the same time that the iceberg detached itself from Win-Dom Glacier, made its awesome plunge into the sea and began its aimless drift down Taku Inlet to the shipping lane of Lynn Canal.

It was just past midnight on the morning of August 15 when the *Islander* dropped the scattered lights of Juneau astern and slashed into the chill bank of fog which masked Douglas Island and the southern mouth of Lynn Canal. The steamer's screws were turning over 104 revolutions to the minute and she was doing perhaps fifteen knots when her slim bows found the drifting iceberg and erupted in a twisted mass of broken steel.

Scottish-built, the *Islander* was considered the finest steamship in the Alaska trade. Her powerful triple expansion engines, driving twin screws, gave her a speed of twenty knots. Although she maintained a fast schedule, she had never been in serious trouble in the thirteen years she had been steaming between British Columbia and Alaskan ports. She was CPN's lucky flagship and people felt safe on her, for even if she should strike a reef or an iceberg everything would be all right. The *Islander's* hull was divided into watertight compartments which could be sealed off at a moment's notice, making her practically unsinkable.

It was two o'clock in the morning when the *Islander* crashed into the berg. The steam whistle shattered the profound silence of the night and the blasts echoed back from the unseen shores and from the great berg. Passengers, those who could, rushed on deck, but many more were trapped in staterooms, for the ship's hull had buckled, jamming many doors tight shut.

Captain H. R. Foote ordered the boats overside when, minutes after she struck, it was evi-

TWO DECADES OF NARROW ESCAPES from disaster on perilous northern sea-lanes caught up with the old Al Ki on May 20, 1917, when she hit the beach at Point Augusta, Alaska. She had escaped from many a similar predicament, but this time her back was broken. The little wooden 200-footer that carried tons of gold from Alaska (and carried news of William McKinley's first election as President to news-hungry Alaskans) was dismantled where she lay. Another old-timer, Excelsior, made the Valdez and Seward run for years under Pacific Packing & Navigation Co. and Northwestern Steamship Co. ownership. In 1906 she began leaking worse than usual; had to be beached at Valdez, below.

Excelsior ashore at Valdez.

PRINCESS MAY REPORTED SUNK IN LYNN CANAL

C. P. R. Boat, Carrying Hundred People, Goes Down

The Seattle Daily Times

ACCIDENT OCCURRED EARLY THIS MORNING

24 PAGES.　　SEATTLE, WASHINGTON, FRIDAY EVENING, AUG. 5, 1910.　　Price 1 Cent. News Stands and Trains, 5 Cents.

C. P. R. S. S. Princess May Lost in Lynn Canal

Wireless Reports Show That Big Ship Met Disaster at 4 a. m. Four Miles Off Sentinel Island---No Word of Passengers and Crew.

BULLETIN—

VICTORIA, Friday, Aug. 5.—The Princess May remained afloat two hours after striking. The passengers and crew were all saved in the steamship's boats. The passengers numbered eighty, the crew thirty-eight.

JUNEAU, Friday, Aug. 5.—The Canadian Pacific steamship Princess May, running between Vancouver and Alaskan ports, is ashore on Sentinel Island, off the coast of Alaska, according to a wireless message received here.

VANCOUVER, Friday, Aug. 5.—It is reported that the Canadian Pacific offices have received word that the Princess May is sinking off Sentinel Island with 100 pas-

PRINCESS MARY PUT ON QUITE A SHOW when, in 1910, she draped herself high on a Lynn Canal, Alaska reef. She escaped almost undamaged. The ancient **Centennial**, opposite page, lower left, went missing for seven years, was sighted, encased in ice, by a Russian Arctic expedition in 1913. The true story of her strange fate has never been explained.

dent that the unsinkable *Islander* was sinking fast. Boats were lowered, but few were filled to capacity. One, with a capacity of forty persons, drifted off into the fog carrying just seven.

Twelve minutes after striking the berg the *Islander* was standing on her head, the ponderous screws still turning madly in thin air as the stern rose high out of the water. Then the dark bulk slid forward, there was a great blast of compressed air from the shattered hull, and the *Islander* was gone. Fifteen minutes had elapsed from the time she struck.

When the death roll of the *Islander* was completed it bore 72 names.

The *Islander* was gone, but certainly not forgotten. Legend had it that she was carrying three million dollars worth of gold when she left Skagway that mid-summer evening, and a lot of people were interested in reclaiming it from the sea. The wreck was first located in 365 feet of water in 1904 and, five years later, the Wiley Brothers of Olympia used a diving bell to bring up about four thousand dollars worth of gold.

Nothing more was accomplished until 1931, when Seattle house-mover Frank Curtis decided to try for the jackpot. It took him three years to do it, but eventually the bones of the

Islander were beached high and dry on Admiralty Island. The salvors sieved through almost a thousand tons of ooze and debris, coming up with a bare $40,000 in gold; not enough to pay the costs of the operation.

On a summer day in 1952 the tug *Donna Foss* completed another routine towing job from Alaska as her crew tied up a bargeload of scrap steel to a Duwamish River buoy in Seattle.

The barge was loaded with the bones of the *Islander*, back in port after more than half a century.

And a month or two after the remains of the Canadian Pacific Navigation Company's *Islander* were cremated in the blast furnaces of Bethlehem Steel Company at Seattle, the 6000-ton Canadian Pacific Railway cruise liner *Princess Kathleen* proved that the passing of half a century had not lessened the hazards of the northern seaways.

On September 7, 1952, the sleek three-stacker crashed high onto a rocky point thirty miles north of Juneau in pre-dawn darkness; later slipped back to disappear in deep water. The *Kathleen*, like the old treasure-ship *Portland*, must have carried a degree of good luck with her, for all 425 persons aboard escaped safely before she sank.

The first recorded shipwreck in the waters of the far Northwest occurred 167 years ago. As this is written, early in 1959, an investigation is still under way as to the cause of the recent sinking of the tug *Henry Foss* in Georgia Strait, with the loss of six members of her seven-man crew.

The final chapter in the story of the northern shipwrecks has not yet been written, nor will it be as long as men and ships pit strength and skill against the hazards of that legendary searoad.

Captain Tom Healy as mate of S.S. Alaska.

tion of wrecked "Princess Sophia" as seen from Vanderbilt Reef.

MARIPOSA sliced off the end of Valdez's fine new city dock in August 1912 when Capt. Moore signaled "full speed astern" and engineer Bent read the order "full ahead." **YUCATAN** was rescued from this 1910 sinking, but she was never the same again. **Northwestern,** below, was also salvaged from this 1910 stranding on San Juan Island.
PRINCESS SOPHIA appeared safe enough after striking Vanderbilt Reef, above, but blizzard and high seas swept her off to drown 343 persons, greatest death toll in West Coast marine history. Only the tip of a mast shows in lower photo.

hwaites. 3106.

AFTER YEARS OF TRANSPACIFIC SERVICE the old **Mariposa** entered hazardous Alaska coast trade where bad luck caught up with her on a foggy night.

Wreck of **Ohio** was, for years, a melancholy landmark along the Alaska coast.

S.S. **Alaska** escaped from this brush with Alaska fir trees and huckleberry bushes.

A **BAD LUCK SHIP** was H. F. Alexander's old **M. F. Plant**. A change of name to *Yukon* should have changed her luck, but it didn't, as the upper photo shows.

Union Steam's **Chelohsin** never recovered from her 1949 stranding either, left, but the **Admiral Farragut**, right, was towed safely home after a minor Puget Sound stranding in 1920.

A VETERAN OF THE WEST COAST SEA LANES was the little wooden 700-ton steamer **Farallon**, launched at San Francisco in 1888 to oppose the powerful Pacific Coast Steamship Company on Puget Sound and Alaska runs. Taken over by Dodwell & Company for gold rush traffic, she passed to Alaska Steamship Company ownership. On January 2, 1910, she left Valdez for Iliamna, crashed into a reef at the head of Cook Inlet three days later. Seas were calm and all 32 people aboard reached shore, where they roughed it, below, while waiting a month for the **Victoria** to come and rescue them.

NORTHERN SHIPWRECKS

Left, top to bottom: **Bertha** was destroyed after 1915 stranding at Uyak Bay, Alaska when water seeped into forward hold, igniting cargo of lime. **Dora** was wrecked on British Columbia coast in 1920. **Kentucky**, purchased on East Coast for Alaska Steam, foundered in the Atlantic, never reached Pacific Coast. **Armeria**, U.S. revenue cutter, fell victim to the dangerous coast she patrolled.
Right, top to bottom: **Al Ki** wrecked at Point Augusta. **Columbia** ashore at Point Wilson, Puget Sound. **Prince Rupert** after striking rock in Swanson's Bay, B.C., 1920.

NORTHERN SHIPWRECKS

Left, top to bottom: **Chelohsin** wreck. **Mount McKinley,** victim of unpublicized wartime wreck on Alaska coast in 1942. **North Sea,** formerly the **Admiral Peoples,** ended her career on reef near Bella Coola, in 1947 while in Northland Transportation Co. service.

Right, top to bottom: **Zapora,** old-time halibut fishing steamer and pioneer ship of Alaska Transportation Company was finished off by this Alaska stranding. **Denali** (1), Alaska Steamship Co. freighter, broken in two on rocks near Zayas Island, 1935. **City of Victoria** on the beach at West Point, Seattle, while on Puget Sound-British Columbia run. **Idaho,** veteran Pacific Coast Steamship northern liner at her final resting place near Port Townsend.

PRINCE GEORGE, Canadian National liner, grounded in fog at Ketchikan in September, 1945. An exploding fuel tank spread flames which gutted the ship, above.
Spokane struck Ripple Rock in Seymour Narrows in 1911; was feared lost, but salvage operations (lower left) refloated her.
Opposite page: Alaska liner **Alameda** in drydock following brush with Inside Passage reef.

CHARMED LIVES seemed led by Alaska steamers, which usually escaped from many strandings and other apparently hopeless predicaments. The Alaska, for instance, emerged from the scrapes pictured above and at the left, to sail tropic seas as cruise liner Mazatlan. Crews grew blasé; sometimes, like engineers Roy Bruce and McGregor, below, considered minor strandings as opportunities to pursue wily Alaska clam with stokehold shovels.

DEATH OF A PRINCESS

The loss of the S.S. *Princess Kathleen* on September 7, 1952, was the most recent and best-remembered disaster to a large steamship on Pacific Northwest waters. It occurred in the waters of a notorious ships' graveyard north of Juneau, not far from where the *Islander* went down in 1901, the Union Steamship Company's *Cutch* sank in 1900 and the *Princess Sophia* slipped off Vanderbilt roof in 1918, carrying all 343 persons aboard to their deaths.

It was three o'clock in the morning when the *Kathleen,* steaming at normal cruising speed through the light rain, struck almost without warning on the rocky shore. The first officer, who had charge of the watch, was unable to explain why the ship was a mile and a half off course.

The SOS was promptly flashed on the air, but on the wrong frequency. After two hours without an answer it occurred to someone to check on the situation and a ship-to-shore telephone call was paced to the Alaska Communications System, after which a nearby Coast Guard cutter hastened to the scene, arriving at 6 a.m.

Although the *Princess Kathleen* remained high on her rocky perch for nearly twelve hours after her stranding, no apparent effort was

PRINCESS KATHLEEN, above, leaves dock for last voyage. The pictures which follow show the chronology of her sinking.

made to seal off her hull from the sea, nor was any of the passenger's baggage removed. At 2:40 p.m. the incoming tide floated the liner briefly, but she filled fast, slipping back until she literally stood on her stern; then slipped under ninety feet of water.

The unhappy passengers filed damage suits for the loss of personal property—clothes, jewelry, watches, luggage, cameras—which all went down with the ship, the claims averaging over

RISING TIDE floats the Princess Kathleen briefly, above. Then, as inrushing water presses down her stern, she slips backward from the rocks and plunges under ninety feet of cold salt water.

a thousand dollars per person. CPR attorneys, however, quoted that interesting provision of admiralty law which limits the liability of ship-owners "to the value of the vessel at the termination of the voyage" (which was zero, since the *Kathleen* was a total loss), plus her "pending freight," which consisted mostly of the fares paid by the passengers for a voyage that was never completed.

Eventually the company refunded the fares paid and settled property losses at the rate of $200.00 per passenger. Although there were those who felt they had received their money's worth in having taken part in a spectacular and much-publicized shipwreck, a good many of the *Princess Kathleen's* passengers view her last voyage, to this very day, as an extremely high-priced lesson in the vagaries of maritime law.

MEMORY OF THINGS PAST

The stirring, colorful era of the coastwise liners has drawn to a close. No more do the white racers *Yale* and *Harvard* knife their jaunty way between Los Angeles and the Golden Gate. The mighty *H. F. Alexander* will never again send the wake of her swift passing hammering against the sea beaches of Washington and Oregon and northern California. The legendary Alaska liners are gone from the searoad that led from Seattle to Nome Roadstead. Steam will not blossom again at the raked crimson stacks of the Union steamers along the Brit-

ish Columbia coast, and even the beautiful Princess liners of Canadian Pacific are little more than ferries now, making day runs on sheltered inland waters.

Sometimes a trans-Pacific liner like Matson's *Matsonia*, pictured above, makes the coastwise run from San Francisco to Seattle before proceeding on a special voyage to Hawaii, but such occasions are rare and, at best, provide only a poignant reminder of days that are past and will never really return again.

◆ THE END ◆

Picture Index